A Daring Journey to Freedom—

Escape from a Japanese Prisoner-of-War Camp

Memoirs of Colonel Gangaram S. Parab, MC

Edited by
Aruna and Shivaji Seth

Never in the field of human conflict was so much owed by so many to so few. – Sir Winston Churchill

Colonel Gangaram S. Parab, MC
(1915–1981)

CONTENTS

FOREWORD

The fall of Singapore to the Japanese army on 15 February 1942, probably Britain's worst defeat in World War II, has been considered one of the greatest defeats in the history of the British Army. The Battle of Singapore lasted only a brief seven days ending in the fall of the "impregnable fortress". It resulted in the largest surrender of British-led military personnel in history. About 80,000 British, Indian and Australian troops became prisoners of war, along with some 50,000 Malayan troops. In 1940, British Prime Minister Winston Churchill had said, "Singapore could only be taken after a siege by an army of at least 50,000 men. It is not considered possible that the Japanese would embark on such a mad enterprise." Later, Churchill called the ignominious fall of Singapore to the Japanese the "worst disaster" and "largest capitulation" in British history.

This book is a profile in courage detailing the daring and perilous war-time escape undertaken by my father, Captain (later Colonel) Gangaram Parab, from the Japanese prisoner-of-war camp in Singapore during World War II. He had written the account of his escape; however, for reasons unknown, did not publish the manuscript. I believe that his story must be told and should take its proper place in the annals of World War II history.

Born on 1 June 1915, Gangaram Parab joined the prestigious Indian Military Academy (IMA), Dehra Dun, India, after completing his studies at the Elphinstone College, Mumbai. In 1940, he graduated from the IMA and was commissioned as a Second Lieutenant, opting to join the 4th Battalion of the 19th Hyderabad Regiment (now known as the 4th Battalion of the Kumaon Regiment). Soon afterward, Second Lieutenant Parab was shipped to Singapore as part of the 12 Indian Brigade. Second Lieutenant Parab, later Captain Parab, fought bravely against the rapidly invading Japanese forces in the Malaya theater of war. He was part of action in the decisive Slim River battle. After the fall of Singapore to the Japanese on 15 February 1942, Captain Parab along with two other fellow officers, Captain Balbir Singh and Captain Pritam Singh, all prisoners of war, undertook the dangerous and courageous escape from the Japanese prisoner-of-war camp in Singapore to return to India. In recognition, the British Crown awarded Captain Parab and fellow escapees each with the prestigious Military Cross (MC) medal for gallantry. Subsequently, during the latter part of World War II, Captain Parab, MC, was part of the military action in Italy and the resulting fall of the Axis countries.

After India's independence in 1947, Colonel Parab, MC, went on to command several regiments, including the 1st Parachute (Punjab) Regiment, the 4th Assam Rifles, as well as several Armed Services Selection Centers with great honor and integrity.

After retiring from an illustrious military career, Colonel Parab, MC, founded and established a cooperative organization to help find jobs for ex-servicemen, including retired officers and disabled soldiers. Today, the Armed Forces Ex-Officers' Multi Services Cooperative Society (AFEXCO) in Pune is a flourishing enterprise that provides diverse services in areas, such as security and transportation. Colonel Parab passed away on 10 July 1981, at the Southern Command Hospital in Pune.

In December 2005, on a visit to Singapore, my family and I

visited the Fort Canning Bunker, where Lieutenant General Arthur Percival (the British General Officer in Command, Malay Command) conducted operations during the battle and fall of Singapore. This bunker housed the Battle Box museum. The Curator of the Battle Box at that time, Mr. Nedumaran, said, "Your father's story has to be told! The spirits of over 60,000 Indian troops cry out for it! The stories of the contributions of all these troops in the Malayan Campaign have been left out of the various post-war histories of newly-independent states."

In October 2010, my husband, Shivaji, and I had the opportunity to visit the Kumaon Regiment Center in Ranikhet, Uttarkhand. We paid an emotional visit to their War Memorial Center, which honored all the brave and gallant soldiers of the Kumaon Regiment in the various theaters of war over the years. The 4th Battalion of the 19th Hyderabad (4th Kumaon Regiment) was honored for the Slim River battle fought during World War II. It was awarded the Battle Honors of North Malaya and Slim River. We wish to sincerely thank Brigadier Jasbir Singh, Commandant of the Regiment Center, for the warm welcome and hospitality extended to us. Some photographs of the War Memorial are included at the end of the book.

During our visit to Ranikhet, we had an unexpected and wonderful opportunity to meet the son of the late Brigadier Balbir Singh, one of my father's fellow escapees from the Japanese prisoner-of-war camp. He has written a book* on the escape of the three prisoners as researched by him, which included referring to my father's unpublished manuscript that had been sent to the Kumaon Regiment Center's Library, and bits of information told to him by his

---

* Brigadier Jasbir Singh, *Escape from Singapore* (Lancer, 2010).

father. This book, however, is a personal account of the escape and journey as written by my father in his own words.

I pay tribute to my mother, the late Mrs. Sulabha Parab, who always supported and greatly contributed to the welfare of the troops and their families during my father's postings to various military stations. I also pay tribute to my brother, the late Major Anil Parab, who also joined the illustrious 4th Battalion of the Kumaon Regiment, and was part of the military action in the 1972 Bangla Desh war with Pakistan and during the insurgency in the Naga Hills area. His life and brilliant army career was cut short in January 1973, when he died in an accident while providing training and instruction to his troops. A brief account of his sparkling and inspiring life, written by our father, the late Colonel Parab, is included as an appendix in this book. I also wish to acknowledge my two sisters, Mrs. Bina Rohatgi and Mrs. Anita Hessenauer.

I wish to dedicate this memoir to my parents' grandchildren—Sameer, Aditya, Malika, Michael and Maria; and great-grandchildren—Alisha, Annika, Sonali, Kaiden, Rania, and Evelyn, so that they may remember their ancestry and know what it means to have courage and bravery in the face of danger and difficult times of war.

Aruna (Parab) Seth
Vienna, Virginia 22182
USA

May 2014

CHAPTER 1
EXPERIENCE IN MALAYA

ON GRADUATING FROM THE INDIAN MILITARY ACADEMY[1] as a Second Lieutenant in April 1940, I opted to join the 4th Battalion of the 19th Hyderabad Regiment[2] ("4/19th Hyderabad"), now known as the 4th Battalion of the Kumaon Regiment, which moved to Singapore as part of the 12 Indian Brigade (the EMU Force[3]). My colleagues at that time remarked that I would never get a chance to fight the enemy in that part of the world, as Japan was unlikely to join in the war. These prophets, like many others in Malaya, were proven wrong. The Japanese entered the war; they dazzled the Allies, and probably the world, with their lightning victory in the East; the myth was exploded.

After the collapse of France and other European countries from German invasions, Japan revived its ambition of seizing the coveted territories of Dutch East Indies, Malaya, Singapore and Burma. With

---

[1] Established in 1932, the Indian Military Academy, located in Dehra Dun, India, is the country's center dedicated to training officers for the Indian military.

[2] The 4th Battalion of the 19th Hyderabad Regiment ("4/19th Hyderabad"). In 1813, Sir Henry Russell, the British Resident in the court of the Nizam of Hyderbad raised the Russell Brigade. Later, this was renamed the Hyderabad contingent and became part of the British Indian Army. The 19th Hyderabad Regiment in 1939 consisted of four battalions: the 1st (Russell's), the 2nd (Berar), the 4th, and the Kumaon Rifles. In 1945, 19th Hyderabad was renamed the Kumaon Regiment.

[3] A key element of British defenses for Singapore against the Japanese forces during World War II. The 12 Indian Infantry Brigade was the main garrison force defending Singapore from the Japanese invasion.

this intention, Japan moved into South Indo-China in July 1941; this was her shrewdest move. It gave Japan a base from which to launch a sea borne expedition against Malaya and its neighboring countries within a short sea voyage. It also brought Japan right up to the frontiers of Thailand, which enabled her to increase pressure on that country. At that time Japan had concluded the Tripartite Pact with Germany and Italy, and was waiting for an opportune moment to seize territories in the Far East.

As relations between Japan and Britain became strained, more troops from India were dispatched to Malaya. The 12 Indian Brigade was one of the first formations to arrive in Singapore, in August 1939. It was entrusted with the task of defending the east coast of Johore State, where the small port of Mersing was thought to be a likely landing place for the invading force, as there were good landing beaches both north and south of the town.

There had been some discussion about the defense of the beaches. One school of thought held that it would be better to keep the beaches under observation only, and to keep the main force concentrated further back, control the communications, and fight the enemy from prepared positions. The other thought was that if the enemy were allowed to land unopposed, it could concentrate a large force to attack the main forces. It would, therefore, be better to hold the beaches as the most likely landing places, so as to hit the enemy where most vulnerable. It would also be easy to combine the actions of the three services to our advantage. It was, therefore, decided to adopt the latter policy with some modifications; that is, to hold the likely landing places in adequate strength with a reasonably strong reserve on the main road to Singapore, which is about 90 miles from Mersing.

Another important town, Endau, situated on the east coast of Johore, is where Japanese owned iron-ore mines. From here a large quantity of iron ore was annually shipped to Japan. We, therefore, had to provide against the possibility of a landing at Endau. Detailed plans were made with the civil authorities for the removal or destruction of all boats and other surface craft from this area.

The work for the defenses of the beaches was completed by the troops themselves. It was easy to dig, but the trenches became water logged quickly and they had to be dug over repeatedly. Barbed wire and other obstacles were erected. The construction of pill boxes along the main road to Singapore was given to a civilian contractor, who in connivance with a British engineering officer made a huge profit providing sub-standard boxes. The British officer was subsequently court-martialed for his part in the scandal.

In East Johore there are large areas covered by jungles of varying types, some dense and almost impenetrable. There are formidable mangrove swamps that only the fittest of men can traverse. Such was the country in which we patrolled and looked for possible approaches the enemy might take! The climate was humid and enervating, and rain fell practically daily.

Jungle warfare is not something that can be learned in a day! It is a matter of several months of hard training. Troops are required to be acclimatized, and strict hygienic discipline must be observed. Still, in spite of the training, men fell ill from malaria and stomach troubles. The important aspects of training to fight in the jungles are the ability to live off the country, and to exist on meager rations and little water. With these things in mind we went on long-range patrols in the virgin jungles. During one such exercise some of the men lost their weapons while negotiating a flooded stream. In the highest traditions of the Indian Army we did not return without recovering the arms.

We came to know this area quite well as we had put in a great deal of effort to build field defenses. When we were quite familiar with our roles, however, the brigade was assigned to Command Reserve and was to be prepared to operate anywhere in Malaya. Rather, the Australians, who had recently arrived, were given the task of defense of East Johore. This was typical of the campaign, as plans were changed frequently.

The Australians were no doubt tough soldiers, some of whom had fought with distinction in World War I. However, in the intervening period between the two World Wars, they had little practical training. The drivers of the Australian transport companies were excellent and they did magnificent work later during the withdrawal of troops. Generally, the standard of discipline, especially saluting, was indifferent, possibly because some of the rank and file had held higher appointments in civil life than had their officers. But on the whole they were a good lot, sporting and friendly.

Malaya is inhabited by several groups, each with its own customs, characteristics, religions, and standards of living. The bulk of the Asiatic populations consisted of Malays and Chinese, approximately in equal proportion. The civilian population, generally, was inclined to be apathetic to war, but helpful to the troops. However, there was a small minority who did not welcome the troops. They preferred to lead a placid and peaceful life, and said that war would never come to Malaya; so why make life difficult?

Malays lived in the countryside and coastal areas, content to live on agricultural produce and fish. Normally they did not like to exert more than what was necessary to subsist; their general attitude was *tidak apa* (carefree and indifferent). Malays were recruited into the Malaya Regiment and other regular units in the fighting services. They were easy-going people who lacked war experience.

In general, the industrious and commercial-minded Chinese lived in the towns. The Chinese were divided into many groups. Probably the most powerful was the one that owed political allegiance to the Kuomintang[4], but the most active and vocal group was the pro-communist. Chinese volunteers, eager to fight the Japanese, generally could not join regular troops in local Army units. Their strengths were more suited to being guides, cooks, and domestic servants. There were a few supporters of the Japanese; they possibly took part in *Fifth Column*[5] activities.

The third largest population of Malaya consisted of Indians, after the Malays and Chinese. The Indians numbered a few thousand, the majority being laborers from South India, who worked in rubber estates, plantations, railways and the Public Works Department. The more educated Indians had professional careers such as lawyers or doctors, or were engaged in trade, while Anglo Indians were also generally employed in white-collar jobs. Indian doctors and lawyers practiced in Singapore and in various other towns in Malaya. Quite a sizeable number of Indians, mainly the Sindhis, owned shops and

---

[4] Chinese Nationalist Party founded in 1912 by Sun Yet Sun. It is currently the ruling Party in Taiwan.

[5] A group of people whose main goal is to undermine a nation from within through clandestine activities such as espionage and sabotage.

were engaged in commerce. The Indian Punjabis, Sikhs and Pathans were in the Malaya Police Force. The Sikhs were especially popular in the police force.

The Japanese owned a number of rubber plantations and iron-ore mines, hair dressing salons and photography studios. In big towns a few Japanese were businessmen, and most good barbers and photographers were Japanese. Their knowledge of the country undoubtedly proved of great value to the invading Japanese forces during the campaign. A number of Japanese had military backgrounds as executives. As service or ex-service men, they were able to organize an efficient espionage system. Thus the Japanese, although small in number, were a constant source of anxiety to civil and military authorities. As the possibility of war became increasingly evident, instructions were issued to our services' personnel to keep away from the Japanese hair-cutting salons and restaurants.

Although in small number, the Europeans, especially the British, were a powerful group. They owned most of the large rubber estates and tin mines. Some of them joined the volunteer corps, but they did not like to be disturbed from their normal vocations. They marred the cordial atmosphere since they practiced color discrimination. Asiatic people, including Indian Army officers, were not admitted to European clubs. Even the British officers of the Hong Kong and Shanghai Royal Artillery Units did not allow Indian officers in their Officers' Mess. Similarly, Indians were not accepted in railway coaches meant exclusively for Europeans. This was one of many grudges harbored by the inhabitants of Malaya against the British, and they wished for a change of masters. Thus the local population had become susceptible to the Japanese anti-British propaganda and took part in *Fifth Column* activities.

CHAPTER II
JAPAN STRIKES

THE BRITISH DID THEIR BEST not to be drawn in a conflict with Japan, but the relations between the two powers gradually deteriorated. Japan increased its activities in the Yunan Province of China to cut the Burma Road being used to bring supplies to China. The applications of drastic economic sanctions by the United States and Great Britain to freeze Japanese assets brought the crisis to a head. It was imminent that Japan would enter the war and attack Singapore. It was, therefore, decided by the Malaya Command to hold an exercise in the Port Dickson area to test its plans to delay the enemy, pending the arrival of reinforcements.

The termination of this exercise, in which the 12 Brigade was acting as enemy to the 11 Infantry Division, coincided with the information that a large Japanese sea-borne expedition was on its way to the Gulf of Siam (Thailand). On the morning of 6 December 1941, a Catalina flying boat that was watching the Gulf of Siam reported to have sighted two convoys streaming westward. Contact with the convoys during the night was lost; therefore, a second flying boat was sent out the following day to ascertain the direction in which the convoys were proceeding. It did not return to base; most likely the plane was shot down.

Under normal conditions, the 12 Brigade would have returned to its permanent peace-time location in Singapore, but the information regarding the movement of the Japanese convoys resulted in the brigade, less one battalion, being ordered to move further north, to the operational location near the Mantein Pass. The battalion left behind was located in Singapore.

My battalion, the 4/19th Hyderabad, concentrated next day in a rubber plantation in Negri Sembilan near the Mantein Pass. At about 2 AM that night (7–8 December 1941), information came through in the form of the code words, *Gloves Off*, meaning that hostilities between the Japanese and the Allies had commenced. Shortly afterwards more definite information was received that the Japanese were attempting a landing at Kota Bharu on the east coast. This information was accompanied by a warning that fire should be withheld should any small boats be sighted, as it was possible that these might contain local fishermen returning to their homes.

That same night Kota Bharu and Singapore were bombed; neither of these cities had commenced observing air-raid precautions, such as blackouts. In Singapore, the local people who heard the bombing thought that normal training operations were being carried out by the troops of the 12 Brigade in that area. Entertainment places like the Happy World and New World, and various clubs were well illuminated. The headquarters of the Civil Air Raid Precaution Organization was not manned, and the lights were on when the enemy planes arrived.

The 4/19th Hyderabad of the 12 Brigade that was in fact the Malaya Command's only reserve, was ordered that night to proceed to Kota Bharu, where the Japanese had landed on the night of 7–8 December. The northern most beaches were manned by the 3/17th Dogras regiment. Confused and fierce fighting developed on the beaches, and losses on both the sides were heavy. Lieutenants Navin Chandra of the 3/17th Dogras and Madappa of the Frontier

JAPAN ATTACKS MALAYA

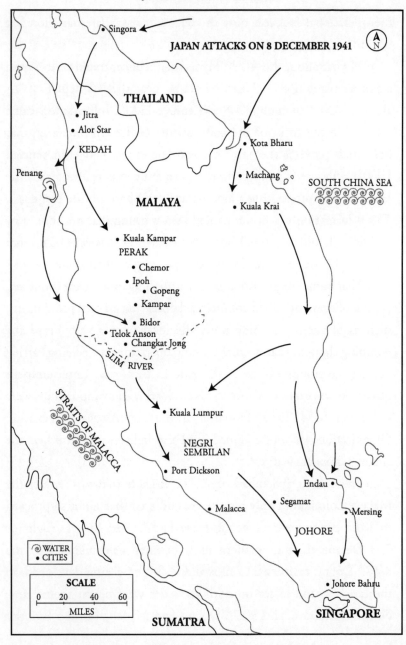

JAPAN ATTACKS ON 8 DECEMBER 1941

Singora

THAILAND

Jitra

Alor Star

KEDAH

Penang

MALAYA

Kota Bharu

Machang

SOUTH CHINA SEA

Kuala Krai

Kuala Kampar

PERAK

Chemor

Ipoh

Gopeng

Kampar

Bidor

Telok Anson

Changkat Jong

SLIM RIVER

STRAITS OF MALACCA

Kuala Lumpur

NEGRI
SEMBILAN

Port Dickson

Endau

Malacca

Segamat

Mersing

JOHORE

WATER
CITIES

SCALE

0   20   40   60
MILES

SUMATRA

Johore Bahru

SINGAPORE

Force Rifles were killed. At this time, battalions of the 8 Brigade commanded by Brigadier Key were deployed on the east coast, with a battalion of the Hyderabad State Forces to defend the Kota Bharu airfield.

The air situation was unfavorable for us. The enemy had established constant fighter aircraft cover over Kota Bharu airfield, making it most hazardous for our bombers to leave the ground without fighter support. Some of our aircrafts were destroyed while others remained grounded; the airfield was abandoned. As a result, the morale of our troops was struck damaging blows.

The move of the 4/19th Hyderabad was carried out by rail and road. On the second day, the unit reached Kuala Krai. The commanding officer stood on the crossroads and commandeered vehicles passing by. He ordered me to take the first party and to move on until the Japanese were encountered. There was pouring rain and visibility was very poor. The enemy was said to be infiltrating in between and behind the fronts. Retreating Air Force personnel were traveling fast and giving alarming news of the fighting.

At dusk when the battalion was about nine miles short of Kota Bharu, it was ordered to stop and take up a defensive position near Keterek. It was expected that those parties cut off and separated from their units when the Japanese landed would be reorganized behind this position. Although the battalion had some combat contact with the Japanese that very night, the general thinking among the troops was that we were still on a training exercise! Heavy and continuous rain fell during the night and it was difficult to prepare defenses in waterlogged ground. However, we were determined to give our best. The following day, 10 December, the battalion was attacked from the air, but suffered little damage. The defensive position was held for about two days. Many small parties of men from the withdrawing 8 Brigade who had been lost or cut off rejoined their units. When orders were received to withdraw, the battalion was given the role of rear guard to the withdrawing brigade.

One significant incident took place in this particular phase of the withdrawal; and many more were to follow when the brigade was moving along the road to a timed plan for crossing a bridge near Machang. A Japanese party got in between the main body and the rear guard, the 4/19th Hyderabad. The main body, thinking that the Japanese would closely follow them over the bridge before the rear guard had crossed, blew up the bridge. In an attempt to prevent the enemy from following them, the main body also opened fire. Unfortunately, that fire was on the battalion position, which caused much confusion. The few casualties suffered by the battalion in this early stage were due to this "friendly fire." Attempts to inform the main body that their fire was directed upon us failed due to the breakdown of our wireless communication equipment.

The night was pitch dark. Our armored cars were brought up and their lights were directed towards the bridge; but this resulted only in drawing heavier fire from the main body. From the volume of enemy fire, it was assessed that the strength of the Japanese was nothing more than that of a "jitter party"[6]. In these circumstances, the battalion had the necessity to remain where it was. In daylight, it would be possible for our main body to recognize us. With improvised rafts and minor repairs to the bridge, the battalion was able to cross the river.

[6] A team conducting combat raids intended to disturb an enemy's repose.

When we were at Kuala Krai to join the 12 Brigade that was engaged in fighting with the Japanese at Cheneròh Lake, we had heard of the sinking of the battleship Prince of Wales and the battle cruiser Repulse. When the news of this disaster was given to the commanding officer, he did not believe it and pulled me up for spreading "rumors." The loss of these great ships cast a gloom over Malaya. Faith was shaken amongst the leaders who appeared to underestimate the enemy. The catastrophe led to the belief in the invincibility of the Japanese superiority.

On joining the 12 Brigade at Chemor, the battalion had a severe setback when the D Company of our battalion, commanded by Captain Harries, was over-run by the Japanese. The overall plan was that the 5/2nd Punjab was to contain the enemy, while the Argyll & Sutherland Highlanders (A&SH or "Highlanders") attack them from the left flank. The D Company was to detour on the right flank to come up behind the enemy. The Punjabis were, unfortunately, unable to contain the enemy and were driven back. The Highlanders could not put on their attack, and the D Company on coming out of their cover was immediately surrounded. This information was given to us by the only survivor to reach the battalion lines. When the Japanese pressure became heavier, the brigade commenced its withdrawal according to the plan.

The battalion rear guard was under my command. One of the tasks assigned to me was the firing of demolition charges previously prepared by the engineers, for blowing the bridges and culverts en route. Owing to heavy rain, the demolition fuses on the second bridge we crossed had become damp, and hence ineffective. The engineers with me, therefore, decided to blow it up with an Air Force bomb. The preparation, however, took some hours and resulted in delay, which caused much anxiety at the battalion headquarters. The bomb was finally detonated and the bridge blown. On rejoining the battalion we heard that the Japanese had bombed Ipoh and the rail communications leading from there.

The 12 Brigade was holding positions at Gopeng. In spite of numerous demolitions, the Japanese continued to advance without respite and quickly mounted an attack that was repulsed. Realizing that the enemy was now in strength, the division commander ordered the brigade to withdraw through the Kampar position and come into reserve at Bidor. It was a daytime withdrawal, a difficult operation that resulted in dog fight. The enemy followed the battalion closely with tanks that produced a demoralizing effect on our troops. The Highlanders who were to follow us started withdrawing along with us. During the confusion, the bridge over the Kampar River was blown up; however, the river being fordable, all managed to get across. Some of the men of these battalions lost their spirit and started swimming in knee-deep water. This shows how easily men can lose courage when in danger.

From Gopeng the brigade was to withdraw to Bidor, behind the positions of the 15 and 28 Brigades at Kampar, for a rest period. The promised rest did not materialize. On the morning of 1 January 1942, seven Japanese steamers accompanied by barges were reported on our left flank on the west coast. The landing at the mouth of the River Bernam was opposed by Malayan Volunteers[7], but they were driven back by the Japanese troops to Telok Anson.

I was detailed as a liaison officer to contact the Malayan

Volunteers who were watching the Telok Anson flank. The motorcycle I was riding went off the road into the river, as the vehicles of the Malayan Volunteers did not give way on the road; the accident left me unconscious. When I regained consciousness, I learned that I was picked up by some of the Malayan Volunteers. Although I sustained some injuries, the motorcycle was not damaged. After receiving first aid and my left arm draped in a sling, I continued my journey on the motorcycle, to contact the retreating forces.

Upon my return, I found that the battalion had occupied new defensive positions along with the 5/2nd Punjab and the Highlanders, about four miles east of Telok Anson. My Commanding Officer, Lieutenant Colonel Wilson Haffenden, was wounded during an air attack while he was going on a bicycle to visit the forward companies. It was known that the Japanese had complete air superiority and no movement of vehicles or troops was possible during the daylight hours. Our commanding officer was of the opinion that the Japanese would not waste ammunition or bombs on a single individual. He, therefore, decided to visit his companies alone on a bicycle, but was singled out by a Japanese aircraft. He was badly wounded and evacuated to Singapore. Lieutenant Colonel Haffenden was a robust officer and a brave soldier, who was prepared to take the risk and face danger. As an individual he was a good person, but as a commanding officer he was not popular. He did not have much skill in handling men, possibly due to his suspicious nature. In the Malayan campaign

[7] As war became imminent in Europe in 1930s, many men from different backgrounds and nationalities (European, Malay, Chinese, Indian and Eurasian) joined the Malayan Volunteer Forces. They received military training at night and on weekends. They assisted the British troops to fight the Japanese.

he did well but did not get any military recognition, as he did not readily commend other's services.

The enemy attacked and heavy fighting took place throughout the afternoon in the Changkat Jong area. One of our men, armed with two-inch mortar, had both his legs blown off. He was in great pain and requested that he be put to sleep forever. But we just could not do that. The entire day we had been fighting practically without any air support. It was most demoralizing to see only enemy planes flying overhead reconnoitering, bombing, and machine-gunning our positions, while none of our planes were in sight.

CHAPTER III
BATTLE OF SLIM RIVER

THE NEXT DAY, 3 JANUARY 1942, withdrawal continued to the Slim River, intended to be the main defensive position for holding the enemy on the main highway to Kuala Lumpur. Once again, the 12 Brigade was ordered to hold the forward positions in this area, while the foremost locality, north of Trolak village, was temporarily held by the 4/19th Hyderabad, until work on the main defensive positions was completed. There was no natural anti-tank obstacle spanning the road. We had, therefore, to depend on artificial obstacles to stop enemy tanks; however, we were not given any anti-tank mines. Only the 5/2nd Punjab, preparing defenses behind our position, was allotted anti-tank mines. The second battalion of the Highlanders Brigade had taken up defense in depth beside the road.

Within two days of taking up defensive positions, the enemy attacked our battalion's A Company. The company achieved great success holding the railway line and inflicted about 60 casualties on the Japanese. Emboldened by this success, the withdrawal of the battalion was postponed; this decision, however, led to a major disaster on 7 January.

The dispositions of the battalion at that time were that the A Company spanned the railway line, and the B and C Companies spanned the road. On the right side of the road, the C Company was commanded by Lieutenant Darling, while on the left side, the B Company was commanded by Captain Gopal Krishna Mehta. The D Company took up a defensive position. The troops had continuously

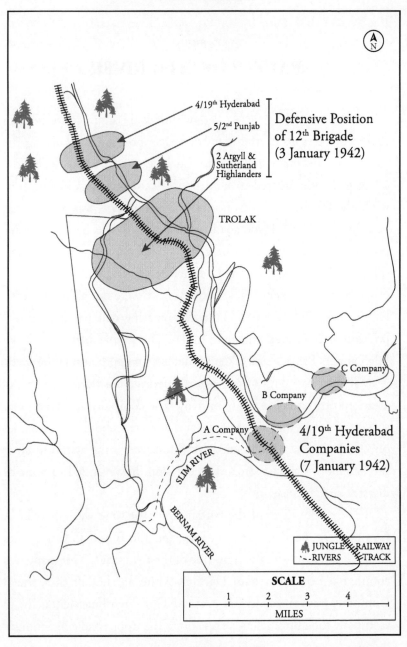

engaged in operations and had no rest since the war in Malaya started. The already tired troops became more tired, as during daylight hours the enemy aircraft constantly hovered and strafed their positions; and at night mosquitoes bit them, so they could not get any sleep.

After the initial setback, the Japanese concentrated all their armor and infantry in strength and relaunched a strong attack against our forward positions during the night. Around midnight a loud rumbling of tanks was heard; which, together with the typical sounds of troop movements, signaled the coming Japanese attack.

The B Company fought gallantly but their only weapons against the tanks were hand grenades and fire bottles; and these, to their great disappointment, failed to stop the enemy advances. There were no anti-tank guns and the B Company's anti-tank rifles also proved useless. This was the unit's first experience against enemy tanks. The Japanese infantry, supported by tanks, went around the Company's area, leading to fierce hand-to-hand fighting. The din that followed defies description! Enemy tanks fired cannons and machine guns while our mortars fired all out. Men threw hand grenades but could not stop the tanks; the grenades merely bounced off the armor leaving the tanks unscathed. The enemy tracer bullets flew all over. The tank crew shouted while engines roared down the road. Our troops were helpless and suffered heavy casualties. This major disaster resulted in the early abandonment of Central Malaya, and thus reduced chances of getting reinforcements.

Captain Mehta was captured, tied up and bayoneted to death, according to the report of a straggler who eventually rejoined the battalion. Lieutenant Vasudeva, the Battalion Motor Transport

Officer heard that fierce fighting was taking place in the battalion area. As he had not received any information about this fighting from the battalion command, he went up the road towards the battalion area to ascertain the facts, only to be met by enemy tanks. Nothing more was heard of this brave officer. He could have stayed behind with the battalion transport, but chose to go to the scene of heavy fighting at the frontline. The fate of Major Brown, who commanded the battalion during this period, was also unknown. We heard that a Japanese tank stood at the entrance of the battalion headquarters, but Major Brown remained calm and steady, issued instructions to the rifle companies to withdraw, as per orders previously received from the brigade. Our losses in this battle were heavy and the battalion was left only with the equivalent of about a company.

Lieutenant Darling of the C Company was reported to have accompanied his men for some days; but later, he was unable to walk due to foot rot, and he insisted on being left in the village of Kampong. Nothing further was heard of this officer.

About 24 Japanese tanks succeeded in penetrating the lines right up to the positions held by the 5/2nd Punjab, leading to fierce fighting at close quarters. Mines laid in front of the 5/2nd Punjab position failed to stop the advancing tanks. The only anti-tank gun of the British Regiment that was deployed by the roadside could not prevent enemy tanks from rushing down the road. Our rear battalions were taken by surprise as the Japanese tanks penetrated deep into the divisional area and inflicted heavy casualties on the unprotected troops. To complicate matters further, no information was passed to the rear due to the poor state of communications. There were no wireless sets; thus units in the rear were unaware of the Japanese breaking through the forward positions. They were completely surprised while performing routine duties in the morning when the enemy tanks came through. The tanks penetrated to a depth of about 15 miles, completely putting the two forward brigades and many supporting arms out of action. Administrative units were also disrupted. Total defeat was averted by hastily bringing in the 155 (British) Regiment with their 4.5 inch Howitzers. The 155 succeeded in destroying some of the Japanese tanks at point-blank range, thus bringing their advance to a temporary halt; but the damage had already been done. The forward brigades, as well as many of the supporting units, were thrown into confusion. The enemy tanks were in possession of the only road that was fit for wheeled traffic, and we had no tanks to counter the Japanese tanks.

This disastrous result was due to various reasons. There was no efficient or adequate anti-tank defense, and communication between the forward and rear troops was unreliable. We had no tanks to counter the Japanese tanks. The enemy's air supremacy added to the physical and mental fatigue of the troops. The troops had been fighting and withdrawing by day and night for a month without proper rest or relief. In the exhausting and enervating climate of Malaya this was too great a test of human endurance.

CHAPTER IV
THE FIRST ESCAPE

AFTER THE SLIM RIVER DEBACLE, I was one of many cut-off from the battalion. As I was the Battalion Signal Officer[8], I knew, as per the plan, that the battalion position was behind the Highlanders. With Jemadar[9] Ram Swarup, the Intelligence Viceroy Commissioned Officer[10] (VCO), and other troops of the battalion, we made our way towards the new battalion position. When we arrived, we found that the Japanese tanks had already reached the area. So we dispersed and tried to reach the divisional area, but getting through the thick jungle was not possible. At the end of the day we did not know where we were. Thus began my first escape adventure! Trekking through the dense jungle we finally came to the Slim River where we divested ourselves of extra items of equipment and clothing, including our pistols that were clogged with mud, and swam across the river. A number of men drowned crossing as they could not swim.

The next morning we met the party of troops led by Lieutenant Colonel Dickens and Major Webb of the 5/2nd Punjab. The party later swelled to about 200 strong, when men and officers of the

---

[8] An officer who is in charge of maintaining communications with key personnel in the battalion.

[9] A rank used in the British Indian Army for a soldier promoted from the ranks, usually after at least 10 years of service. This is the lowest rank for a Viceroy Commissioned Officer.

[10] Indian soldiers promoted from the ranks usually after at least 10 years of service. Viceroy Commissioned Officers were the principal link between the Army's mostly British officers and the sepoys (soldiers).

Highlanders joined us. That night we managed to get some rice from an abandoned house. With great eagerness we boiled it in an empty tin can, but shortly we were very disappointed. It was a kerosene tin can, so we could not eat the rice though we were very hungry! Eventually, we left the place without any food but with charged tempers.

There was only one route to follow in the direction of our forces that were supposed to hold Kuala Lumpur until 15 January 1942. It was, therefore, decided to cross the road during the night. The party was divided into three groups: reconnaissance, main body and rear guard. As the youngest and most junior officer, I was put in charge of the reconnaissance group leading the column. No sooner had we approached the road, the Japanese directed the headlights of their vehicles on our party. Immediately everyone disappeared into the jungle leaving the leading group of three, including me, in the center of the road! It is a mystery as to why the Japanese did not open fire on us; hereafter, we met no one from the rest of the column.

With me were the driver of the Brigade Major[11] and a clerk from a Gurkha battalion. We took to the jungle where we spent the night. We were wet as it rains constantly in that part of the world during the months of December and January. To keep off the mosquitoes, which were very troublesome, we tried to smoke them away by burning pieces from our shirts and trousers. We fought a losing battle and eventually lost our uniforms. The next day we climbed the tallest tree in the neighborhood to try to ascertain our exact position and to locate a village or any other form of habitation. As luck would have it, a rubber

[11] The Chief of Staff of a brigade, whose role was to expand, detail, and execute the orders of the Commanding Brigadier.

plantation was seen half a mile away, to which we made our way through the jungle.

The Tamil laborers, although in a state of terror at the collapse of the once mighty British power, fed us whatever food they had. We did not reveal our identity to them at first, but they must have guessed that we were soldiers from the marks on our legs, which were derived from the hose-tops and *puttees*[12] that we wore in those early days of the war. We found the marks most difficult to hide during our later adventure. After having enjoyed the hospitality of the laborers, we made our way further south towards Kuala Lumpur. That night we slept in a hut, whose only occupant was an old Chinese, who neither asked any questions nor opposed our entry as he was not in a fit state to do so. Our slumber was disturbed by the chattering of Japanese soldiers who approached the hut; so we quietly crept out of the hut and made our way through the darkness to sleep outdoors under some trees.

The scorched earth policy followed by our troops was restricted primarily to roads, bridges and materials that might be of value to the enemy. Unlike the Russians, it was not applied to things such as food, water, and modern necessities like electric power supply. This otherwise would have given ground for Japanese propaganda against the British. We had expected that extensive demolition of bridges would impose considerable delay on the enemy, but this was far from what happened. In fact, the Japanese were very quick and efficient in repairing bridges and overcoming obstacles throughout the campaign.

[12] A long strip of cloth wound tightly and spirally around the legs. This was adopted as part of the uniform for soldiers in the British Indian Army.

Next morning we followed a railway track going towards Kuala Lumpur; but unfortunately, we bumped into a party of Japanese, who were going around the village collecting people to work on repairing a bridge that had been demolished by our retreating troops. As we were without uniforms, we were included in one of the village parties sent to work on the bridge like other civilians. Towards the evening I pretended to be suffering from diarrhea and was allowed to break off from the group and go into the jungle to ease myself. I repeated this several times, so that the Japanese would not suspect that I was shirking work or planning to run away. When it was getting dark, I asked once again for permission to go behind a bush; once there, I ran as fast as I could and hid in the jungle. The Japanese made no attempt to pursue me and I continued my journey alone. Although my two companions knew my plan, they did not try to escape with me and I do not know what happened to them. To be alone at night was frightening; but to cope with this fear, I continued to walk along the railway tracks that provided direction towards my destination.

Early in the morning of the following day, I was in Kuala Lumpur; but to my horror, I found that the town was already occupied by the advance elements of the Japanese mounted on bicycles. Pillars of smoke and flames rose into the sky as vast numbers of military and civil stores, rubber factories, mine machinery, and petrol and oil stocks were set on fire. There were abandoned cars, destroyed houses and bomb holes in the streets. No usual crowds of chattering Chinese and Malay were to be seen. The town was deathly silent; the streets deserted. The civil population had either disappeared into the jungles or left hurriedly for Singapore. It was a distressing sight. Only the Japanese were to be seen, busy scavenging choice articles of food, clothing and attractive items, such as watches and pens.

Being very tired and hungry, the sight of a bicycle left by a Japanese soldier, who was engaged inside a shop, tempted me strongly; I picked up the bicycle and rode away. The presence of Japanese soldiers everywhere put a stop to my further progress along the road. I therefore made my way towards the railway yards through a drain. I had to get across the river, but our retreating forces had demolished the bridge. As my hand was injured, it became difficult to carry the bicycle; however, I managed to get it across with help of the girders and railings hanging from the demolished bridge. After crossing the bridge at about 9 AM, I lost no time in proceeding to the place where I hoped to find our troops. By 6 PM I had covered roughly 28 miles, traveling towards Singapore. I could see traces left behind by our retreating troops, but did not know when or where I would be able to contact them again.

On approaching the Mantein Pass, I saw some marks on the road, which to my mind, looked like mines laid by our troops. However, as I was going downhill without having to pedal, I did not bother to dismount from the bicycle to find my way through the mines. Going up the hill, I had to walk, as I was not strong enough to pedal up the steep grades. At the top of the pass I noticed some movement; and before I realized what was happening, soldiers with fixed bayonets surrounded me. Both the soldiers and I were pleasantly surprised to recognize each other as members of the same unit. I was moved by the warmth and affection shown by the men, but I could not stay long with them to eat purées that they so quickly cooked. The Divisional Commander urgently required seeing me as I was the only person who had come back through the Japanese lines after the Slim River debacle. The experience of escaping through the enemy occupied area, even though it was only for a short duration of five days, was most thrilling. It gave me the satisfaction of having rejoined my battalion. Thus, my first escape came to an end.

CHAPTER V
THE BATTLE OF SINGAPORE

I REPORTED TO THE 11 DIVISION HEADQUARTERS, where I stayed the night and related my experiences to the General Officer Commanding, Major General Paris, who earlier commanded the 12 Infantry Brigade. Next day, after a de-lousing treatment, medical examination and a good bath, I was at lunch in the 3rd Indian Corps Officers' Mess at Segamat, when a Japanese aircraft bombed the area. Every officer present, without any thought for his dignity, immediately went to ground under dining tables and chairs. Fortunately, not much damage was done, except that a portion of the mess building was blown up and a good deal of debris was scattered on the officers.

Later, I was put in an ambulance train going to Singapore. On the way, a few Japanese planes flew low over the train, which immediately stopped. The crew and the staff sought cover in the nearby jungle leaving the wounded and other patients in the compartments. I considered that the comparative comfort of my berth was better than what I would find in a ditch or in the jungle, so I stayed where I was. In fairness to the Japanese, it must be said that the train was neither strafed nor bombed, although most of us expected an attack.

During this phase of the operation, my battalion was assigned the responsibility for the close defense of the Johore – Singapore causeway, which was being prepared for demolition. I was commanding the forward company on the bridgehead. At dusk on 30 January 1942, an ambulance driver reported to me that he was looking for Lieutenant General Sir I.M. Heath, the 3rd Indian

Corps Commander. The Commander had come in May 1941 from the Middle East where he had commanded the 5 Indian Division in the battle of Keren and subsequent operations in Eritrea. He was a veteran of the First World War who enjoyed considerable reputation in the Indian Army. The driver's inquiry made me anxious, as we had not received any news of the General having been wounded. I rang up the battalion headquarters, which was also not aware of the reason the ambulance was sent. However, later it was learnt that the General wanted to witness the demolition of the causeway that was to be demolished early in the morning the next day. He had, therefore, decided to spend the night in this ambulance.

The causeway was a massive concrete structure, carrying both a road and a railway line. The Island of Singapore is separated from the mainland of Malaya by the Straits of Johore, across which the only permanent connection was the causeway. It was 1100 yards long and 70 feet wide at the water line and much wider below it; its demolition, therefore, was a very difficult task. Considerable protective measures were taken near the causeway to ensure that debris from the explosion did not injure the troops in the vicinity. The last of our troops from the mainland crossed the causeway at the crack of the dawn without an incident. What an opportunity the Japanese had missed! Immediately after the last of our troops, the Highlanders, had crossed over, everyone was warned to get down into specially prepared deep trenches. The blowing up of the causeway was a sight to remember. There was a flash, followed by a deafening sound accompanied by smoke, almost sky high, and dust everywhere. A breach was made in the causeway, and water rushed through a gap of about 70 feet. Sappers (engineers) then filled the gap with a barbed wire obstacle,

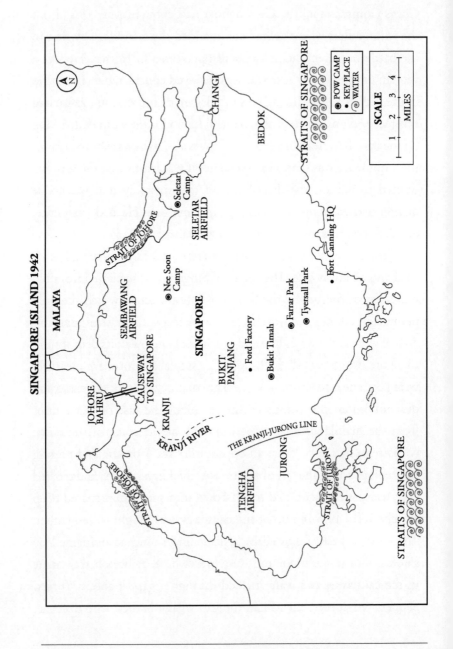

SINGAPORE ISLAND 1942

making crossing impossible.

Thus ended the retreat from the mainland of Malaya and the battle for Singapore began. The whole operation seems incredible: 550 miles in 55 days, forced by a small Japanese Army of only three or four divisions. It was a war of patrols getting around our positions and sitting on a road behind our troops, thinking that if we were cut off we would retreat.

By the time I reached Singapore, the brigade, including my battalion, had been pulled back to that town for reorganization; and we went into our old camp at Tyersall Park. Here, a large draft of three officers and 200 men joined the battalion that was now commanded by a Major from the 1/19th Hyderabad. Once again we were earmarked as the command reserve brigade for the defense of the island of Singapore. The final withdrawal of all troops from the mainland of Malaya was completed on the night of 30–31 January.

The defenses of Singapore Island had been laid out before the outbreak of war primarily to repel an attack from the seaward side, the southern coastline of the island. These fixed defenses could not be moved easily to meet a land attack from the north. It was a bitter blow in that they were never to be tested against a sea borne attack by the enemy. In fact no proper defenses were constructed on the north and west coasts of the island where the Japanese made initial landing. This was the subject of much critical comment on the failure of the British Army and the success of the Japanese strategy.

On 5 February, the Japanese bombed Singapore Island and information was received that the Empress of India, a troop transport vessel, had been bombed and sunk by the same planes that had taken part in the bombardment of the island. This ship was bringing reinforcements to Singapore. On 8 February, the battle of Singapore started. The enemy brought a large number of guns for this attack. Around 10 AM the Japanese heavily shelled the west coast where the Australians were holding the position. Shelling continued to increase in intensity until midnight, when the enemy landings started on the same coast. The situation was confused and it was most difficult to know what was happening in that area, as communications with the forward troops had been disrupted by the Japanese shelling. The forward defenses were flattened and the first flight of the enemy troops came across the Straits of Johore in special armored landing crafts. Many of them were sunk or driven back, but others came on. Thus, the Japanese got a footing ashore at many points. Some of our beach searchlights were destroyed in the bombardment and others were never exposed, probably due to fear of drawing artillery fires. The mounting of this operation by the Japanese across the water obstacle in a space of about a week was a very fine military performance. The 12 Brigade was ordered to move forward to Bukit Panjang village to help the Australians. The brigade concentrated in that area by mid-day of 9 February. Even though there was much enemy air activity, casualties were negligible early on; however, the casualties were very heavy later in the day.

All officers of the battalion collected near battalion headquarters for orders. The Brigadier and the Brigade Major also came to see if there was anything they could do for the battalion. As it was evident that we would soon be launching an attack, we decided to eat the haversack lunches we carried. While we were in the process of offering our lunches to each other, enemy bombers came down suddenly and bombed the area. Many casualties were inflicted. The petrol storage in the nearby rubber plantations was hit and the exploding barrels were thrown high in the air. The explosion of these barrels in the midst of the troops added greatly to the casualties and the prevailing confusion. Dead and wounded were lying everywhere; the place was in shambles. Due to this severe setback, our planned attack did not take place.

In order to stabilize the front, the battalion was ordered to take up positions near the Kranji Jourong line. On 10 February, more Japanese troops landed near the mouth of River Kranji. This meant that the troops on the Bukit Panjang road were in danger of being cut off. That night the oil storage tanks on the island were opened and set on fire in the hope that the burning oil would be carried down the river and would spread in the midst of the Japanese crossing it. Some damage may have occurred, but it certainly did not stop the enemy. In the morning, we were amused to see that our faces were completely covered with soot and burned oil! Many of our troops looked more like miners coming out of a coal mine than fighting soldiers. It was difficult to maintain self-control under these conditions. Some of the British and Australian troops were very critical of their government, and they did not spare even the King for the failure to make adequate preparations for the war. They asked where the Hurricane planes were that were going to sweep the air. The stragglers or groups of men detached from their units were very bitter about the series of disasters.

The Japanese brought in their tanks on the Bukit Timah Road and confused fighting ensued. No orders could be passed to the companies in time to withdraw due to the failure of communications. The commanding officer called the officers he could reach, and told them to make their way, along with their men, towards the position on the Bukit Timah Road. We were not quite certain whether we would come out safely from that battle, so we finished whatever drinks we had in the officers' mess and carried the remaining bottles in our haversacks. On our way at night we had to pass the 12 Brigade headquarters, near which a Japanese tank had taken up position. The Brigadier told the Brigade Major to investigate the cause of the nuisance on the road. The Brigadier Major immediately took a lantern and started off with the intention of "telling off" whoever was responsible for the noise as he thought it was a carrier of our own troops. No sooner had he presented himself in the open, he was greeted with a burst of machine-gun fire. Fortunately, he was not hit, and the Brigadier realized that it was more than just a nuisance. He coolly put his cigar in his mouth and said, "Boys, things are getting too hot around here, let us get out." In the confusion that resulted, Captain Jilani, the Adjutant, and I fell into a deep pit full of ordure. The more we struggled to get out, the deeper we sank in. It was nothing short of a miracle that we eventually came out! We were also fortunate that we escaped sure death because a hand grenade exploded nearby. After this the battalion once again found its way back to Tyrsall Park to defend its own barracks, as was also the case with many other units.

The next day this area, including the 12 Indian Brigade's General Hospital, was heavily bombed. The hospital, in a hutted camp, suffered a great deal. In fact, the hospital proved to be a death trap, as casualties who could not be moved owing to leg injuries burned to death. The surgeon, Major Kapur, calmly continued with his emergency operations in spite of the bombing and burning of a major portion of the hospital. As the hospital was in the center of the military camps and Singapore city, its bombing could have been more inevitable than intentional. In one trench, seven people, including the Subedar Major[13] of the battalion, were killed by enemy shelling. Our camp, which consisted of *atap* huts[14], was subjected to aerial bombing and artillery bombardment, which destroyed the battalion's band equipment and the silver in the officers' mess. Many harrowing tales came out of this fighting. For cold-blooded barbarity, very few nations can surpass the Japanese. For instance, Havaldar[15] Bishvember was bayoneted by the Japanese and left for dead. Passing Japanese soldiers used him for bayonet practice. Remarkably, he remained alive in spite of these serious injuries.

On 12 February, the defense perimeter was made smaller. The following day, the battalion was told to submit the names of officers who were not in command of troops, and who were considered to be expert in jungle warfare. They were to be sent back to India to train troops in jungle warfare. An officer from our battalion serving on the staff as Brigade Major was selected, and he joined those going back to India. Unfortunately, the ships were either bombed and sunk, or captured by the Japanese and brought back to Singapore. Consequently, the officers, nurses and doctors could not return to India. Among these officers was Major Bahadur Singh, later (after the war) to become Lieutenant General. They all spent the rest of the

[13] Rank used in the British Indian Army for a senior Viceroy Commissioned Officer.

[14] Huts made with Atap palm leaves for the roof and wattle for the walls. A traditional housing found in Malaya and Singapore.

[15] Rank of a Viceroy Commissioned Officer equivalent to a sargent.

war in captivity.

With the defense perimeter shrinking daily, the Indian National Army[16] (INA) troops contacted Indian troops to persuade the men to surrender and join the INA. The INA was an armed force formed by Indian nationalists in Southeast Asia in 1942, during World War II. The aim of the INA was to liberate India from the British occupation with Japanese assistance. At the outbreak of World War II in Southeast Asia, 70,000 Indian troops were stationed in Malaya. After the start of the war, Japan's spectacular Malayan Campaign had brought under her control considerable numbers of Indian prisoners of war; nearly 55,000 after the fall of Singapore alone. The conditions of service within the British Indian Army, as well as the conditions in Malaya, had fed dissension among these troops. From these troops, the First Indian National Army was formed under Captain Mohan Singh. It received considerable Japanese aid and support.

---

[16] The Indian nationalist force formed during World War II, whose aim was to overthrow the British rule over India.

CHAPTER VI
CAPTIVITY

ON THE MORNING OF SUNDAY, 15 FEBRUARY 1942, a strong rumor circulated that we would surrender by that evening. When the white flag signaling surrender went up in Singapore's fortress area at Fort Canning, orders were issued that the cease-fire would be effective from 8:30 PM. That day came to be called the Black Sunday. A few minutes before the cease-fire, Captain Jaswant Singh was wounded by enemy shelling. I was in the same trench, but escaped unhurt. By 8:30 PM all fighting had ceased and quiet descended on the bomb-scared town. All communication with Singapore was severed and the disastrous campaign was over. We felt sad. That night nothing of importance happened except that the cease-fire signal came through on the air-raid sirens.

Talks between the Japanese commander, Lieutenant General Yamashita, and the British General Officer Commanding (Malaya), Lieutenant General Percival, took place at the Ford Factory on the Bukit Timah road, where the Japanese later erected a Victory Monument. It is said that this monument was later destroyed when Singapore was recaptured by the Allied Forces. After the cease-fire, very few men had a clear idea about what was to happen to them or about what they were supposed to do as prisoners of war. That night, some soldiers who had money rolled the notes into cigarettes and smoked them quite happily. That same night Captain Hussein, Captain Balbir Singh and I thought about escaping, but we thought that it would be unwise to attempt a get-away while firing was still going on and the Japanese were on alert. The next day we were told to dump our weapons for the Japanese to collect; however, the quantity of weapons was so great that it was impossible for the enemy to collect them all. The Japanese were not organized for this purpose.

All European prisoners (British and Australians) were to march the next day to the Changi area, while the Asians were to assemble at Farrar Park. This was the first step by the Japanese towards imposing a color bar, which was not practiced openly in the Army but was freely followed in civilian life. (For example, Asians in Malaya and Singapore were not allowed to join European clubs; this was a sore point for them.) Prisoners were ordered to take only the clothing they wore and two rations of food. After wishing farewell to the British officers, we marched off in different directions on 17 February.

At the time of the capitulation, the combined British, Indian, Australian, and Malayan forces in the Singapore fortress area numbered approximately 85,000. This figure includes a large number of administrative troops and non-combatants, who were inadequately trained to participate in combat, as well as recently arrived and very poorly trained reinforcements. Had they killed even one enemy between four of them, the campaign potentially would have been prolonged. But mere numbers do not decide the fate of the battle; many other factors are of vital importance. In order to be effective in modern war, the force must be integrated, well balanced, and supported by aircraft and armor.

On arrival at Farrar Park, all Indian, Malayan and Chinese prisoners of war were paraded in front of the pavilion. Colonel Hunt of the Cavalry, who had commanded the Reinforcement Camp, handed over the prisoners, including officers, to a Japanese

Intelligence Officer, Major Fujiwara. The Japanese Major made a short speech in Japanese, which was translated into English and Urdu by Lieutenant Koniska and Lieutenant Colonel N.S. Gill, respectively, and broadcast via loudspeakers. Major Fujiwara said:

> In ten weeks time the Japanese mighty armed forces conquered Malaya and the invincible fortress of Singapore; and the British Empire is dwindling down. Japan is fighting to free the Asiatics from the domination of the Anglo-Saxon race and to form a greater Southeast Asia co-prosperity sphere under the leadership of Dia Nippon. For this purpose, Japan wants to drive out the English from India and wants the cooperation of all Indians. The Japanese had no design on India as General Tojo had already declared. It was a shame that 400 million people should be slaves of 45 million people. If all the Indians were to cooperate sincerely in achieving freedom for India, the English could be driven out without shedding any blood. Remember, Asia for the Asiatics. We are not going to treat you as prisoners of war, but in such a way as to help us get freedom for India. From time to time you will be asked to provide working parties and you should not object to this work. The Japanese have no design on India. In fact they are grateful to her as the Lord Buddha was born in that land.

Later Major Fujiwara handed over all the prisoners of war to Captain Mohan Singh, who was the originator and founder of the INA. This officer had been serving with the 1/14th Punjab regiment in Malaya and was captured during the early encounters with the Japanese in north Malaya. He told us how he contacted the Japanese and how he had formed the INA. He said that, in fact, he was never captured. After he had spoken to the Japanese officers he thought that it was a golden opportunity for India to achieve independence with the help of the Japanese. In his speech, he brought out many instances of the ill treatment given to the Indians by the British, especially with regard to pay and allowances, color bar, and the disparities in various privileges. He also recalled that the Indian troops were always put in front lines; and when they withdrew under enemy pressure, they were shot from behind by the British troops, especially in Singapore.

Mohan Singh was followed by Giani Pritam Singh, a civilian, who had accompanied the Japanese from Bangkok. He, with his volunteers, went around our front lines calling on the Indian troops to surrender to the Japanese and thus save their lives. He now appealed to all the Indians to work for the movement and for the independence of India from the British Empire.

After the public speech making was over, Major Fujiwara called all the officers into the Park pavilion. They were offered Australian brandy, which was, of course, from stocks captured in Singapore. While drinking, Major Fujiwara asked the officers to ask questions for clarification, and also invited them to have a free discussion with him on any subject. He again stressed that it was a shame that 400 million Indians were dominated and enslaved by a mere 45 million British. He reiterated that if all of us cooperated with them, India could become free from the British control without shedding a single drop of blood. After this, the ceremony was over, and all the troops were told to go to their assigned camps.

I came to know that prisoner of war camps were established at the following places:

Place:	Administrator:
Seletar	Lieutenant Colonel Ushaq (Hyderabad Infantry, India State Force)
Bidadari	Lieutenant Colonel Nagar (RIASC[17])
Tyersall Park	Lieutenant Colonel Gurbux Singh (Jind State Force)
Buller	Major Phadnavis (4/19th Hyderabad)

[17] Royal Indian Army Service Corps.

Tengha Airfield	Major Ghanshyam Singh (RIASC)
Kranji	(Not Known)
Bukit Timah	(Not Known)
Nee Soon	Major Shah Nawaz (1/14th Punjab)

My battalion was allotted an area in the Nee Soon Camp. These were the barracks of the Hong Kong and Shanghai Artillery Regiments that could accommodate only about 1,000–1,200 men, but now were required to hold about 22,000 prisoners of war. All the sick and wounded that had been in hospital were brought to the camp, because the hospital buildings were taken over by the Japanese for their own use. Our rations were getting short. The Japanese were not particular in providing rations; in fact, they did not make *any* arrangements. Water was also scarce. Due to congested conditions and low vitality of the troops, diseases like dysentery spread like wildfire, and flies bred in the thousands in the camp. Men died every day. While the doctors did their best, they were handicapped by lack of medication. However, the small stock of medicines they had did save the lives of a great many men.

A deep trench around the camp, dug by the prisoners, was intended to prevent them from escaping, even though the Japanese guarded the camp. The Japanese looked down upon their captives; this was mainly due to the fact that the Japanese themselves did not like to be taken prisoners and they naturally despised those who seemed content to be captured. They showed no respect for the ranks of the officers. Soldiers and officers were put in the same camp; however, the former officers' bungalows were allotted to officer prisoners. No one was allowed to wear badges showing rank.

All prisoners, including officers, had to do fatigue work. The

Japanese treated us as coolies. If prisoner performance was not satisfactory in accordance with the ideas and expectations of the Japanese in charge of the work, the usual punishment was slapping or bayoneting. Japanese beating of the prisoners was a normal occurrence. Any Japanese soldier was allowed to slap the face of any prisoner of whatever rank on any pretext. Protests were not only ignored but invited more beatings.

Later on, the Japanese took movie pictures of the prisoners, obviously for propaganda purposes, either to boost morale at home by showing the number of prisoners captured, or to show the world how well the prisoners were looked after. Propaganda lectures were also part of prison life. There were no newspapers available, and rumors like, "Americans have landed on the Singapore Island" were rampant.

An Administrative Committee of Indian captives was formed in the camp, subject to general directives from the Japanese. Lieutenant Colonel N.S. Gill, 4/19th Hyderabad, was named the Administrative Commandant. Members of the Committee included: Lieutenant Colonel Gilani from Bhawalpur State Force; Lieutenant Colonel Chatterjee, Indian Medical Service; Lieutenant Colonel Bhonsle, 5/18th Garwal Rifles; Major Kiani, 1/14th Punjab; Captain Hussein, 4/19th Hyderabad (assistant to the Commandant); and Captain Kashyap, 15 Field Company Madras Sappers (engineers). Their work was purely administrative; all the orders came from the Japanese through Captain Mohan Singh.

As the food situation was becoming critical, the Japanese, after great persuasion, agreed to provide some rations. I was detailed to collect the rations, taking vehicles to the Bukit Timah Rubber Factory, where our old rations were dumped. I was told to collect permits on my way at the Japanese headquarters that was on Stephenson Road. I entered the headquarters with great difficulty because the sentries could not understand my language, aside from their lack of respect for the Indians. When I eventually arrived before an officer, I saluted him smartly; but this was taken as an insult. He became furiously enraged and I thought that it was the end of my life. However, the sentry at the entrance of the office promptly pulled me back, threw away my head dress, and pushed me in again, saying that I should bow to the officer, not salute. The officer prisoners had to bow to even the Japanese sentries. This illustrated the characteristic attitude of the Japanese. Everything possible was done to humiliate the officers. It was unpleasant, but we had to adjust ourselves accordingly.

The stock of rations had sunk to such a level that it was pitiable to see healthy men being reduced to mere skeletons. When the doctors complained that food of insufficient calories was being supplied to the prisoners and that there was a general shortage of milk, sugar and medicines, the Japanese made a very generous offer of some buffalos that had been brought from Australia, and even suggested that we milk them.

A hospital was improvised in ordinary rooms of barracks. It was soon full, then overflowing. The doctors were the busiest people in the camp. They did magnificent work and saved many lives in spite of shortage of equipment and medicines. Naturally, the morale was low but *esprit de corps* kept us going. Captain Dhargalkar (later Lieutenant General) and Captain Hari Bhadwar (later Major General) were segregated in a separate room, probably for ridiculing the Japanese or the INA personnel. We were worried about their safety but fortunately no harm came to them.

The normal routine in the camp was fatigue work. Once when Captain Balbir Singh went out with a party to load trains, he managed to smuggle a case of brandy into the camp. This was a great boon to all of us and kept our spirits high, especially when dysentery was prevalent. At times, some Japanese, depending on the situation, were quite helpful. A Japanese soldier once became friendly to me after I offered him a sweet cup of tea. The next day he brought a pig and a shirt for me. We did not kill the pig immediately, wanting to keep it in reserve for a rainy day. Unfortunately, we soon lost it either because of our carelessness, or the pig bolted away to save its own life, or someone else had a grand feast on it!

After some days, various parties were detailed to go to Borneo, New Guinea, Thailand and places in Burma to work on airfields, railways or roads; or to assist the Japanese in carrying loads. The 4/19th Hyderabad party was detailed to go to Borneo, but Captain Balbir Singh managed to get the order canceled through the influence of Lieutenant Colonel Gill. Instead, the battalion was sent to the Bukit Timah camp in Singapore.

Up to that time none of the troops in Nee Soon camp had joined the INA, even though the normal propaganda lectures and talks continued. Most of us did not really know where we stood. We asked Lieutenant Colonel Gill for his advice, but were diplomatically told not to worry, and to carry on as we were. The words seemed so familiar to many of us: "don't you worry your little heads." Although he did not join the INA openly, Lieutenant Colonel Gill was undoubtedly the brain behind much of their organization. He was active in trying to improve prisoners' conditions. Lieutenant Colonel Gill was a Sandhurst Military Academy[18] product and was respected by all the prisoners of war. He wielded some authority with the Japanese, and on many occasions obtained immediate results from his interventions. He lectured the officers on the necessity of discipline, the dignity as prisoners of war, and saluting and living with honor. Unfortunately, the reality was that prisoners had no honor or dignity left.

On 11 March, Captain Balbir Singh and I were detailed to take a working party of men from our battalion and 11 Division General Purpose Transport Company, from the Nee Soon camp to the Bukit Timah camp. The Japanese gave us a very circuitous route to follow against our wishes, possibly because they were suspicious of our intent. The Japanese generally were very secretive and did not believe in others. It was amazing that they succeeded in carrying out their plans in operation. Secrecy seemed to be bred in them. It was almost impossible to get any Japanese soldier to give any information. At times they carried the secrecy to an extreme. Japanese soldiers overseas were practically cut off from any communication with their families at home.

When we reached the Bukit Timah camp, we were told to establish ourselves near the Bukit Timah quarry. Our task was to break stones and carry them to the Tengha Airfield, where an additional runway was being constructed. Altogether we had about 1,100 men in this camp. Living conditions were worse than in the Nee Soon camp. Mosquitoes were as big as flies. Although there were

[18] The Royal Military Academy Sandhurst (RMAS) is the British Army Officer training center.

no regular guards in the camp, the Japanese living in the Bukit Timah village patrolled the area.

The routine administration of the camp, subject to the directives from the Japanese, was left in the hands of the senior prisoners-of-war officer. This was because first, the Japanese did not want to tie down their fighting strength; and second, they had no ready organization to deal with the prisoners of war. They announced that any men caught trying to escape would be executed. Rations provided were insufficient, so prisoners were given a reduced bare minimum. Only rice was provided, which was not adequate. Consequently, the health of the men started deteriorating. This in turn decreased the output of work, which was not liked by the Japanese. They slapped, kicked, and even bayoneted anyone not found to be working hard. This made the officers' position awkward, because they were unable to redress the grievances of their men. Men were becoming weaker day by day and were finding it difficult to march back to the camp after work. It was revolting to see the men being beaten like cattle.

During this period, we heard from the local civilians that the Cripps Mission[19] had arrived in India with an offer to give Dominion status to India. At times we would get local newspapers (that were controlled by the Japanese) through Indian civilians, and so obtained some news. In addition, the Japanese published their own paper

---

[19] The mission sent by the British government to India in 1942, which was headed by Sir Stafford Cripps to negotiate an agreement with the nationalist leaders, such as Gandhi (Congress) and Jinnah (Muslim League), to secure full cooperation and support for Britain's efforts in World War II. In exchange, Britain promised full self-government after the war. Both the major parties rejected this proposal, the Mission proved a failure, and no middle ground was found. Congress and Gandhi did not wish to support the war efforts and demanded immediate independence for India.

called Nippon. When in a good mood, they would give us a copy of it, but the news was stale and full of Japanese propaganda. There were no letters from home, nor were there arrangements to send our letters, as no Red Cross personnel were permitted to visit the camps. We wondered whether we were forgotten.

We had been very eager to know the news of the outside world. We did not have any radio sets with us. Even civilians were not allowed to listen to the British Broadcasting Corporation[20] (BBC) news; but they did so at great personal risk. They were allowed to hear only the Japanese broadcast. There were two conventions that governed the treatment of prisoners of war: the Hague Convention of 1907 and the more far reaching Geneva Convention of 1929. Japan was a signatory of the former, and although her representative had signed the latter, it was never ratified. The Japanese, therefore, would not admit any responsibility to follow the Geneva Convention. We were dealing with an enemy who observed the rules only when it suited.

It may be interesting to know that stories of inefficiency of Japanese soldiers and airmen, emanating mainly from Hong Kong and the mainland of China, had been accepted at their face value in Singapore. It was believed that the Japanese couldn't shoot straight as the majority of soldiers wore glasses. The Japanese airmen were considered to be poor pilots. The Japanese military prowess was underestimated, as the Japanese were unable to subdue the Chinese. It was perhaps because of these factors that very little effort had been made to study the potential enemy. The belief that war with Japan was unlikely also had its effects.

[20] British Broadcasting Corporation was the premier radio station providing news during the war.

When we were working on the Tengha airfield, the Japanese stationed at the airfield organized the birthday celebrations of their Emperor Hirohito. I and a few others were called to a feast where we were offered Japanese wine. Later, we were taken to the town and shown a Japanese propaganda film. The Japanese soldiers went to the pleasure houses in the town, which were reserved for their exclusive use.

As mentioned earlier, on the night of the surrender of the Singapore garrison, before we went into captivity, Captain Balbir Singh had suggested that he, I and some others should try to escape and get back to India. He was keen that I should associate with this adventure as I had previous experience of escape. We had thought this over and decided that it was not advisable at that time, as everything was topsy-turvy and shooting was taking place indiscriminately. We revived those plans. Our idea was to get a boat or *sampan*[21] to make for the nearest island first; and somehow get to India later. However, it was very dangerous to go near the coast, especially in the harbor area. We, therefore, postponed this plan for the time being.

A number of events took place during the months of February and March. We were told that Captain Mohan Singh and his friend Captain Akram Khan had gone to Tokyo, the latter with some other Indian civilians from Malaya, Borneo and Thailand. Captain Akram Khan and his companions were all killed when their aircraft crashed on the way. The India Independence League[22] was established with branches in Java, Sumatra, Borneo, Thailand, Malaya and Burma. Attempts were also made to establish and expand the INA from

---

[21] A Chinese flat-bottomed wooden boat.

the Indian troops taken prisoners and from civilian volunteers from Malaya and neighboring countries. Before the capitulation of Singapore a nucleus of the INA had already been formed from the troops captured in the early stages of the campaign. They had camps at Ipoh, Kuala Lumpur and in Singapore. The INA camp in Singapore was called the *Volunteers Camp*, mainly made up of men captured on the mainland of Malaya. Prisoners of war who were in Singapore at the Alater, Bidadari, Tyersall Park, Buller, Tengha Airfield, Kranji, Nee Soon and Bukit Timah camps were also asked to join the volunteers for INA.

A few days later a lecture was delivered by Captain Mohan Singh to the officers at Bidadari Camp, explaining the objectives of the INA. The gist of the address was as follows:

Japan only wants India to be free. Great Britain will never give India independence. They have made promises in the past but have not fulfilled them. We feel hurt when we see a big country like our India with its great and ancient history dominated by an Anglo-Saxon race. We, therefore, want to end their rule. Japan is indebted to India for the culture given to her. Lord Buddha was born in India and Japan wants to repay her debt by helping Indians to get their independence. Now is a golden opportunity, and if we fail to seize it, it may not come again. India expects that every one of you does his best in this struggle for freedom. The British treat us as slaves and we must drive them out from our mother country.

The speech was well delivered and most appealing. Shortly

[22] A political organization operated to organize those living outside of India into seeking the removal of British colonial rule over India. Founded in 1928 by Indian nationalists, the organization was located in various parts of South-East Asia and included Indian expatriates, and later, Indian nationalists in-exile under Japanese occupation. During the Japanese Occupation in Malaya, the Japanese encouraged Indians in Malaya to join the Indian Independence League.

thereafter, Captain Taj Mohamed, DSO[23], MC[24], and a Major from the Bahawalpur State Force came to the Bukit Timah work camp to enlist volunteers, especially from the officers.

The idea of joining the INA did not appeal to some officers, VCOs and others for various reasons. It was not that these men were less patriotic than those who joined the INA, but their inherent instincts were repelled by the way the INA and its affairs were conducted. The INA gave commissions and positions of command to the junior Non-Commissioned Officers[25] (NCOs) of the Army and inexperienced VCOs. The discipline of the INA troops was most unsatisfactory; and above all, the obvious Japanese domination of all INA activities led to the belief that the INA was merely a puppet organization that eventually would serve only the interests of the Japanese. They were also convinced that the attainment of freedom through the methods adopted by the INA would be neither correct nor effective. They considered that the best that could be achieved by such methods was merely to change masters. They felt it was much better under the circumstances to keep the "known devil," rather than the unknown. Therefore, it was decided that their best line of action would be to remain as prisoners of war until they were released.

[23] Distinguished Service Order. A military award of the British Crown for distinguished service by officers of the armed forces during wartime, typically in actual combat.

[24] Military Cross. A prestigious medal awarded by the British Crown for acts of exemplary gallantry during operations against the enemy.

[25] Ranks not commissioned in the Army, but which formed the "backbone" of the army. Senior NCOs were considered the primary link between enlisted personnel and the commissioned officers in a military organization. Their advice and guidance was particularly important for junior officers, who began their careers in a position of authority but generally lacked practical experience.

In those days we had to deal with several officers at the INA headquarters at Mount Pleasant Road, where Captain Mohan Singh and his staff worked. Captain Mohan Singh was styled as the General Officer Commanding of the INA even though he did not wear the badges of a general. Captain Mohan Singh gave the impression that he believed in the movement of the INA as he sincerely felt that he was in it to liberate India; but at times he seemed to be dissatisfied with the Japanese domineering attitude. He probably was suspicious of the Japanese genuineness towards India's freedom.

Captain Mohan Singh's staff included regular commissioned officers from the Indian Army, as well as a number of ex-Indian Army NCOs promoted to the rank of officers. Akram Khan, of 1/14th Punjab, was Mohan Singh's right hand man. Second Lieutenant Rattan Singh, a civilian, who claimed to be a descendent of the Rathore family from Rajasthan, was the Aide de Camp (ADC) to Mohan Singh. Also on the staff of the INA headquarters were Second Lieutenant Sadhu Singh, from 1/14th Punjab, originally an NCO, and Captain Allah Ditta of the Mountain Artillery, who was earlier a VCO.

As already mentioned, I had to visit the INA headquarters on a couple of occasions in connection with getting rations for the men at the Bukit Timah and Nee Soon camps. All of the staff were extremely friendly and hospitable, and gave me expert's advice on how to get things done by the Japanese. They also assisted me in getting some clothes, which came very handy when I eventually made my escape. Unfortunately, one of the sarongs that I collected was of the type normally worn by women; even so, I wore it frequently.

As time went on working at the Tengha airfield, rations became scarcer, but fortunately, the Japanese were not eating the stocks of atta (wheat flour) they had captured. It was therefore given to us in small quantities. Men were falling ill due to poor nutrition and lack of medical care, which naturally hurt prisoner productivity. This displeased the Japanese and they beat the men severely in our presence. Although we were officers, we could not do anything to help our men and naturally felt very small in front of them. We, therefore, thought that it would be much better to escape to get out of our helpless position, though at one time we felt that loyalty to the men demanded that we stay with them. We started making plans for our escape.

Whenever we went out in working parties, we met the Australian and British prisoners of war, but the Japanese did not like our talking to them. Those who were in the habit of smoking or drinking were really in a difficult and pitiable state. They improvised cigarettes from the local tree leaves. If by chance, civilians passing by threw some cigarettes or *bidis*, either as a gesture of good will or to taunt the prisoners, there was a scramble to pick them up, which usually resulted in the cigarettes or *bidis* being smashed. We were told that the rations given to the Europeans and the Australians were slightly better than those given to us. However, they were handicapped since they did not know how to cook rice; they used too much or too little water so that the cooked rice generally was unfit for consumption. We gave them demonstrations whenever we worked together. They were also rapidly losing weight, but their spirits seemed high; true to the old British sense of humor, they were perpetually joking. The British soldier at the best of times heartily disliked *fatigues*[26],

[26] A soldier's work uniforms.

and he therefore loathed the work he was required to do. He did just enough work to keep out of trouble. On the other hand, the Japanese appreciated the Australians for their hard work. We also had opportunities of watching them at work when they were at the Bukit Timah Ford factory. This place was selected to erect the Japanese victory monument for two main reasons: first, it was the place where Lieutenant General Percival surrendered to Lieutenant General Yamashita; and second, it was supposed to be the geometrical center of the island. The monument was constructed with the labor of the prisoners of war.

At times, we felt that the better treatment meted out to the white prisoners, such as organizing their camps, giving them transport to carry their rations, etc., was possibly due to the fact that the nations to which they belonged otherwise would raise inquiries regarding any bad treatment. In our view, the prisoners from countries considered important received consideration that was not accorded to the Indians. This was good enough reason to convince anyone that, should the Japanese win the war, the Indians would get worse treatment than they did under the British rule.

CHAPTER VII
PREPARATION FOR LIBERTY

AT THE BUKIT TIMAH CAMP, we were reinforced by another batch of officers and men. Initially, there were only two officers in the camp, Balbir Singh and myself, but later Captains Phadnavis, Dilkhushman, and Ramaniah joined us. The newly arrived officers were senior to both of us. The Japanese, therefore, started giving orders through them for the next day's work. This gave us an opportunity of not coming in direct contact with the Japanese. Our plan for escape was thus precipitated by the arrival of these officers.

The rail traffic from Singapore to the mainland was about to be opened for civilians. Because of the shortage of accommodation and food on the island, people were told to return to their homes, and for this purpose were issued permits by the India Independence League. However, only Indian civilians who had registered as members of the League were given the permits by the League's branch. One day, when Balbir Singh and I were in the city on fatigue duties, we managed to enroll as members of the League and obtained membership cards.

Captain Pritam Singh, another prisoner at the Bidadari Camp, originally from the 4/19th Hyderabad and later serving with the 3/16th Punjab, contacted us. We knew that he too wanted to make his way back to India; and when we mentioned our escape plans to him, he readily agreed to accompany us. Pritam Singh was able to contact us frequently through Lieutenant Colonel Nagar, also previously of the 4/19th Hyderabad and later transferred to RIASC, who was on the Administrative Committee of Bidadari Camp.

ESCAPE ROUTE

We discussed our plans for escape with the officers who were with us in the camp, but all advised us against escaping. Once I went to the Nee Soon Camp to ask the advice of Lieutenant Colonel J. K. Bhonsle. He also was against it, and very strongly advised me not to be so stupid as to leave the camp. However, we did not give up the idea. Our main problem was to raise sufficient funds. This was becoming difficult as the local prices of essential commodities were rising daily. Fortunately, Balbir Singh and Pritam Singh had some friends in Singapore, such as the proprietors of Rose and Company, who gave them some money. One of the Subedars in the camp, Trilok Singh, gave us 60 Indian Rupees. In all we managed to collect about 200 Straits Dollars (Malayan). We also managed to make some sort of civilian clothes out of a salvaged tent. I was lucky enough to find a straw hat in one of the disused camps. We acquired a map showing Malaya, Burma, Thailand and India, and I cut out the portion giving the land route to India and concealed it in my hat.

There were two possible routes of escape, one by the land and the other by the sea. The land route went northwards through Malaya, Thailand and Burma to India, a distance of more than 3,000 miles. Compared to this the sea route was much shorter, but it was not used by any civilian shipping companies because of the uncertainty of voyaging on the seas. We had even explored the possibilities of making our way to one of the neighboring islands, but we were not certain of getting a boat capable of a long sea voyage. The land route, besides being the longer, was through the most difficult terrain. However, as the fighting was going on in Burma, we thought that the Japanese would not suspect that we would try to escape by the land route. Moreover, the refugees from the mainland were allowed to go to the northern parts of Malaya, and the sale of rail tickets to the public had started. Therefore, we considered that taking the land route would be feasible. We decided to join the refugees and make further plans en route.

As mentioned earlier, the people we consulted in the matter of escape discouraged us from this venture. One of these, Lieutenant J.B.B. Garewal of the 5/2nd Punjab, in Seletar Camp, who had been born and brought up in Burma, also advised us against this attempt as the land route was dangerous. We however knew that Indians were to be found in almost every town in Malaya, Thailand and Burma; and we felt that it would be possible to make our way over land to India with their help. It was clearly understood by us that if we were caught, the Japanese would kill us. For this reason, we changed our names: Balbir Singh would become Bhajan Singh, Pritam Singh became Balwant Singh, and I became Prem Singh, which was actually the name of a cricket batsman. We made up good cover stories to tell if we were questioned; that we were clerks employed on a rubber estate and were proceeding to join our parents.

Our routine daily work would start at about 6:30 AM and conclude at 5:30 PM, with a two hour break at 10 AM. All the officers in the camp would sit together and discuss our escape plans. The outcome of these discussions was always disheartening. They would say that it was foolhardy to try to escape to India. If caught, there was no hope of survival and no one would know how or where we died; whereas, if anything happened to us in the camp, someone would be able to tell the story of our death. There was also a feeling among many officers that any successful escape would lead the Japanese to adopt even stricter security measures and step up the maltreatment of prisoners. However, Captain Phadnavis, who was the senior-most officer in the camp, said that he would give us a clear lead time by concealing from the Japanese the fact of our escape for at least 48 hours. The daily camp routine required the senior-most officer to check the presence of all personnel in the morning before starting work and at the end of the day's work, and report to the Japanese whether everyone was present. Once when Balbir Singh and I were in charge of the men, we allowed one of our VCOs, Subedar Dewan Singh, who had joined the battalion on the Island as a reinforcement from the 1/19th Hyderabad, to escape. No report of his absence was made for about a week. We considered that it was the duty of every person taken as a prisoner to help any colleague who genuinely wanted to escape. A man who had the guts to risk his life deserved all sympathy.

We were becoming physically weaker day by day as every one of us was suffering from dysentery, malaria, or some other disease. Therefore, after having made some provision for clothes, money and medicine, we decided to attempt our escape at an early date, 4 May 1942. The camp doctor, Captain Ramayya, managed to spare some quinine tablets for us, although he was short of them. We told most of the VCOs and NCOs that we were going to attempt an escape.

At last the long awaited day dawned. Parting with our old companions was heart-rending. There was a lump in my throat and we all literally wept at the thought that we might never meet each other again; it was a moving scene.

We slipped out of the camp in the evening, one by one, taking with us the good wishes of our companions, both officers and men. We were dressed in civilian clothes and carried small bundles, each containing a sheet, blanket, towel, and other small necessities. Balbir Singh and Pritam Singh went out first, followed shortly by myself. We went along the railway line, and after a while reached the Bukit Timah – Singapore Road, where the other two officers got into a taxi and went straight to the railway station. I joined them at the station, which was crowded with refugees trying to go to the mainland.

There was not much difficulty in obtaining tickets as we were holding membership cards of the India Independence League. The cards indicated that we were clerks working on a rubber estate. The reason for leaving Singapore showed that we were going to join our parents in Penang. We had no definite plans regarding the specific route we would take, but we would make decisions en route depending on contingencies as they arise. We bought our tickets for ten Straits Dollars each to Prai, the terminus of the train we took. The train was crowded with refugees. We got into one dark corner of a compartment but were slightly separated from each other. The train left Singapore in the evening, and went very slowly over the portion of the blown-away causeway that had been repaired with tree trunks. All the time we had feelings of anxiety and were nervous and suspicious of everyone around us. Whenever anyone looked at us or spoke to us, his intentions were suspect.

During the night Balbir Singh developed a high fever, but we did not wish to stop anywhere for fear of being recognized and losing the chance of getting away by the train. There was not much food at any of the stations, but due to our eagerness to escape we did not really mind the discomfort. We did not get a wink of sleep. The next morning we were very tired. The following afternoon of 6 May, we reached Prai, where we bought tickets for Alor Star, arriving there at about 7 PM. We had never before been to that town, but we had made inquiries on the train about whether there was any Gurudwara[27] and where Indians lived.

On arrival we went straight to the Gurudwara that was a short distance from the station. As Balbir Singh was very ill by this time, we decided to stop at Alor Star to give him a chance to recover. The next day, he was taken to a hospital staffed by Indians and Eurasians. He remained there for a few days and was treated free of cost. Balbir Singh recovered gradually but was not getting strong enough to walk. Therefore, the only course left to us was to continue our travel by train into Thailand, which would not be possible unless we were in possession of passports. Our intention was to get into Thailand before the onset of the rainy season.

Living in the Gurudwara we gathered more information from three local men, Bishan Singh, Gurdit Singh and Dogar Singh, about the conditions on the border that was about fifteen miles away. Dogar Singh, a former Public Works Department employee, who had been reinstated in his job by the Japanese, advised us that the best way to get out was to go to Penang and get a pass to enter Thailand from the Japanese, through the India Independence League Office. After a few days we went to Penang. At the government office we met a Sikh clerk who, on hearing our request, told us to see him the following day. We stayed in a Gurudwara that night. The next morning we were given passes in English and Japanese, valid for three months, to visit our relatives in Bangkok, Thailand.

In Penang, we met a Sepoy (soldier) from our regiment who

[27] A place of worship for the Sikhs. However, all faiths are welcomed in the Gurudwara.

had been captured earlier on and was now selling sweetmeats and pakoras. He told us that Subedar Dewan Singh, also from our unit, who had escaped from the Bukit Timah Camp about a fortnight before us, was now in the INA camp in town. We went there to speak to him. He told us that it was not possible to cross the border as it was heavily guarded; he tried to dissuade us from attempting to return to India. We asked him to accompany us but he refused. We also had interest in the money that we knew he had. He probably suspected our motives; therefore, he neither accompanied us nor parted with his money.

We also met two officers, Second Lieutenant Mathur, RIASC, and Second Lieutenant Trilokekar, Indian Signal Corps, and Sepoy Risal Singh. One of their party members, a VCO, had gone back to Singapore to obtain some money from a south Indian relative. On his return they planned to hire a country boat to go to Victoria Point in Burma. At first we thought that we might as well wait and join them; but on reconsideration, felt that the group would be too large, making it difficult to escape without attracting trouble. Since we all liked the idea of going by sea from Penang to Victoria Point, we investigated the possibilities, but found that no boatman was willing to take us there. Later, we thought that we should buy a sampan and go by ourselves, but the cost was exorbitant. Meanwhile, the sea was getting rougher each day as the monsoon was approaching. The idea of going by sea was therefore abandoned and we returned to our original plan of going over land.

Trilokekar was keen to come with us, but he was in a dilemma, as we could not wait till his VCO's return from Singapore, nor could he leave the party with whom he had originally planned to escape. (Later, on our arrival in India, I visited Trilokekar's parents and gave them his news. His fiancée, who had been anxiously waiting for his return, was very happy to get his news. Subsequently, I learned that Trilokekar was killed. What a tragedy!)

We returned to Alor Star and again contacted Dogar Singh, who took our passes to a Japanese officer. The passes had to be endorsed by a representative of the Thailand Government's authority. However, the following day, Dogar Singh informed us that because of some disagreements the Thai authorities were not accepting passes issued by the Japanese. He also told us that to cross the border and travel in Thailand we were required to possess not only the Japanese pass, which we had, but also the Thai passport costing about 210 *Ticals*[28], which we did not have. Now we did not know what to do and returned to the Gurudwara. We were left with little money, a problem that disturbed us greatly; therefore, we started a small business selling fresh fish, vegetables and fruits at some profit. This enabled us to buy a few essential articles such as mugs and a cooking pot for making rice and boiling tea, whenever available.

While staying at the Gurudwara a tragic incident happened, which compelled us to move on. A Sikh policeman, returning from his duty at dusk, had to pass a Japanese sentry posted near the Gurudwara. Local Japanese orders required that anyone who passed a Japanese sentry had to salute. The Sikh did not salute the sentry, probably thinking that he was not required to salute anyone after the retreat, reverting to the custom of the British days. His failure to do

---

[28] Reference to the Thai currency, Baht, by the English speaking people.

so was taken as an insult by the sentry, who shouted at the policeman and brought him to a halt. The sentry tried to slap the six-foot tall Sikh, and when that attempt failed miserably, he tried to kick the Sikh. This was greatly resented by the Sikh policeman who, in turn, slapped the sentry. The sentry rolled over three or four times. The struggle was seen by other Japanese soldiers; they rushed to the rescue of their comrade. They surrounded the Sikh, tied him to a telegraph post, and bayoneted him to death. Even after he was dead, other Japanese who were not involved in the original melee, tried their bayonets on his corpse.

On 22 May, we decided to proceed further, despite the fact that our permits were not properly endorsed. Before leaving Alor Star, Dogar Singh had given us a letter of introduction to his friend, also a Sikh, named Gurpal Singh of Kongein, Thailand. We left by rail for Padang Besar, a village just on the frontier of Thailand. On reaching Padang Besar we were searched by Japanese soldiers and Thai police, who took away whatever stock of quinine was left with us. After the inspection of our permits we were allowed to proceed by train to Haadyai Junction. We got off the train at Koge, a few stations short of Haadyai.

Thailand was the only country in Southeast Asia which was not under colonial rule. The Thai people in villages lived simply and worked like the Malays, just enough for their livelihood; therefore, outsiders such as the Chinese and the Indians did well there. The Thais were ordered by their king to wear European dress but it was not very popular with them. Their teak wood houses normally were built on stilts along the banks of rivers or rice growing plains, which flooded during the monsoon. Rivers were used for shipping rice to the market, and for bathing and drinking water. Rivers also provided fish, the Thais' principal protein source. Fishing nets suspended from bamboo and lowered into the river were a common sight in the rivers. During this part of the journey we lived on boiled rice and fish. Our difficulties in Thailand were mainly due to the fact that we did not have proper permits to be in Thailand, we did not know the Thai language, and we were constantly worried about being caught.

We contacted Gurpal Singh the following morning and gave him the letter from Dogar Singh. This gentleman introduced us to a bullock cart owner named Ujjagar Singh, who took us in his cart loaded with hay to Haadyai where we arrived at about midnight. This journey was specially arranged to avoid close scrutiny at the immigration office on the road; and as we approached it, we covered ourselves with hay. We froze when we heard the voices of Japanese guards at the border crossing; there would be no chance to escape if the guards had checked under the hay with their long bayonets.

In Haadyai, we could not get anyone to stand surety for us, nor did we have the money to get passports from the immigration authorities. Eventually, on the advice of a doctor named Pillai, a local of Haadyai, we decided to board the train without the Thai passports and run the risk of being found out. We bought our tickets separately and sat in separate compartments as we thought that at least one of us might be lucky to avoid detection. In Thailand no trains for civilians ran during the night; therefore, we spent most of 25 May in Bandon, about 12 miles from Surastra Dhani, at the home of a local Sikh resident, Santokh Singh, who received us very well and laid out a sumptuous meal — our first good meal after a long time. The host watched us with amused benevolence as we greedily ate the delicious fruits, parathas with butter, and other items. We also carried away some food with us for the next day's travel.

The following day, we went on, again by train, to Chumphon, and stayed in the house of Labh Singh. By this time we had made a practice of finding out the names of the people who were likely to help us by inquiring on trains from fellow Indian travelers, or at the various places we stayed. At Chumphon we were told that the route we proposed to take to Victoria Point would be difficult, as there were a number of Japanese check posts and Victoria Point itself was heavily garrisoned. Labh Singh, therefore, advised us to take either the Prachuap Khiri Khan – Tenasserim route or the Bangkok – Sawarnalok route to Burma. He thought the Prachuap route had very difficult terrain, as it went through a dense jungle, but there was less chance of being caught by the Japanese. Other routes were said to be slightly better but we would more likely encounter the Japanese.

We decided to take the Prachuap route and proceeded the next day to Prachuap Khiri Khan. Here we stayed at the house of Khan Zaman, a meat seller, for about four days. He was a thin, elderly, gray-haired Pathan, banned from India for having murdered a Marwari in Calcutta. On coming to Thailand, he had married a local Thai girl and was doing a roaring business by selling meat. In Thailand most people were Buddhists; they did not kill animals for food themselves, but they ate meat from animals killed by others. During our stay at Khan Zaman's place we were fed very well, especially meat. Even though we were suspicious that we were eating beef, we had no alternative. In return for his hospitality, we worked in his cattle sheds and slaughter house, and even carried the meat to the bazaar. To swell his profits, Khan Zaman bought cattle "lifted" from Burma at very cheap prices. These cattle trails were the only known tracks across the border. We tried unsuccessfully to get a guide to take us along this jungle route.

Khan Zaman had two or three servants to look after the cattle. One of them was a Madrassi (South Indian) Mohammedan known in Thailand as Kaka. He was not happy in the service of the tough Pathan, who was really a hard taskmaster. So, when he learned that we were planning to go to India, he volunteered to go with us. He told us that another servant of Khan Zaman, a Thai, knew the route and could guide us. Looking at this offer as a God-sent help, we agreed, even though we felt a certain disloyalty to our host, who had looked after us so well for the last several days. Circumstances being desperate, we preferred to abide by the saying, "all is fair in love and war." Since we were at the last known habitation until we crossed well into Burma, we laid in provisions of Shakapara biscuits, rice, salt and a cooking pot.

Early one morning we asked the servants of Khan Zaman to take the cattle out into the jungle. Once we were in the actual jungle, the Thai servant, who had claimed that he knew the trail into Burma, confessed that he did not know the route. We sent him back to Khan Zaman. We also told Kaka to return, but he refused. We felt that his going would invite trouble from Khan Zaman; however, we consoled ourselves with the thought that Khan Zaman himself was ill that day and his son had already gone to the bazaar for selling meat.

Without a guide it was difficult to find and follow the correct route; sometimes we went round in circles. At night we reached a small village and stayed in a hut. Seeing our bundles, the villagers thought that we were carrying valuables, which they seemed anxious to obtain by getting rid of us. We had to remain on our guard throughout the night. Unknown to us, the tribes of that area were hostile to us. As we did not know their language, we would have faced great difficulties had we encountered more of them.

Early next morning, we left the village and carried on through the jungle keeping our general direction westward. Our plan was to get to Burma by the shortest route. This journey, however, proved to be more hazardous than we had expected. Our pace was, of necessity, very slow and it was not long before we reached the middle of a dense forest. As we marched further the density of the forest increased. Animal tracks, especially of elephants, were frequently seen. These tracks created a great deal of confusion as to which path to select. Our difficulties were further aggravated as the sun could not be seen through the dense growth and clouds; the monsoon was approaching. We went ahead not always sure whether we were going in the correct westerly direction.

After marching for a while the monsoon broke, and whatever trail there might have been was obliterated by the rains. The Tenasserim region gets more than 200 inches of annual rainfall. We were absolutely drenched to the bones and leeches became a source of much inconvenience and annoyance. A halt under a tree would bring innumerable leeches clinging on to us. We carried on in this fashion throughout the day and stopped in the evening. We constructed some sort of shelter with sticks and leaves and managed to boil some rice, though it was difficult to find dry firewood for cooking fire. Although we were very tired, we could not get sound sleep because the cold was intense and our clothes were wet. The danger of wild animals was also there, so we tried to keep a fire burning to scare them away. In the middle of the night we heard a large number of elephants feeding on bamboo clumps nearby. We dared not make a move lest we attract their attention, which would have resulted in damage to our shelter and possibly to ourselves.

Early the next morning we hurriedly prepared our meal of boiled rice and tinned fish. After eating we started moving again without knowing whether we were on the right track. After some hours, possibly around midday, we saw about a dozen cattle and buffaloes being driven towards Thailand by four men. The haste with which they were moving gave us the impression that they were, in all probability, cattle lifters. This gave us some consolation that we were on the right track, knowing that cattle from Burma were smuggled into Thailand. However, the cattle lifters pushed us roughly against the trees, and then searched and warned us. We tried to talk to the men to find out where we were, but they did not answer our questions.

We were still in the virgin jungle; and getting through remained difficult with no trail to follow. We were not sure whether we would ever get out of the forest. At Khan Zaman's house we were told that it would take us about two days to get through the jungle. We had, therefore, taken provisions for two days only as we wanted to travel as light as possible to enable us to move swiftly through the jungles. We were now getting really worried as our rations were coming to an end. We could not sleep at night due to our worst enemies — the mosquitoes and the leeches. Our stock of salt was very low, as it was all used for smearing on the exposed portions of our bodies to help keep us free of leeches. We also cleared the ground at all the rest-stops and rested on raised platforms to avoid the leeches. We often regretted for having selected this route to reach Burma. Our regret was not so much for the hazards of the journey, but more for the possibility that we might perish in the jungle.

The third day's journey was a repetition of the first two: jungle, sleepless nights, mosquitoes, leeches, uncertainty and rain! On the morning of the fourth day, we found ourselves in a state of great depression. The strain, anxiety for safety, and tiredness was very much reflected in our dispositions. We blamed each other for having taken this route, even though it was selected after much thought and examination. It had turned out to be far more difficult than we had expected. At midday we halted to ascertain our position. We were all in a pathetic state of mind and brooding over our plight, when an unexpected incident took place: we heard the call of a bird for the first time since we entered the jungle. I knew from the familiar call of the bird, "tee-tee-tee", that it was one that always lived near human habitations! We were convinced that a village must be nearby. We started our march again and, after a short distance, we heard the tinkling of a cowbell, followed by dogs barking. This cheered us up immensely. In great jubilation we continued to walk towards the familiar sounds. Sighting us, a dog bounded up to us barking ferociously; we thought that the brute was going to attack us. Meanwhile, the villagers were alarmed and ran towards us with dahs, sticks and other weapons. They thought that we were probably cattle lifters or robbers, who were taking advantage of dusk and had come to their village to do some harm. We hoped that, after having put up with so much hardship and longing for the sight of human beings, we would not be killed by the very first people we met! To our good fortune, a Burmese who knew some Hindustani came to our rescue and saved the situation. After this the villagers, though primitive, were most kind and hospitable. They gave us a meal of rice and some form of curry. For a while, we thought of staying in this village, Tabolik, which is near tin mines; but being on the Burmese/Thailand border, we considered that it would be much better to get away from the border. We had reached Tabolik on 5 June.

CHAPTER VIII
IN BURMA

THE NEAREST TOWN IN BURMA WAS MERGUI, and the journey there was by no means easy. The southern part of Burma (Tenasserim) is densely forested, and parallel hill ranges run from north to south. Rice is grown in the narrow valleys; the rice fields get flooded during the monsoon. Valleys are intersected by tidal creeks and mangrove swamps up to three feet deep. There are few trails going across the hills. The monsoon having set in, traversing the steep and slippery paths, most of them obliterated by the rain, was arduous. We were getting physically weak with each day's march, and there seemed no end to our marches. There was no alternative; we had to either go on or perish.

After four days of strenuous marching we reached Mergui. This is a fairly large town on the west coast, where there was a large number of Indian businessmen, mostly from the Marwari community. At Mergui, we were checked by a Burmese Police Officer, who passed us as employees of the derelict tin mine called Tabolick Tin Dredging Company. We stayed in a Gurudwara and reminisced with much satisfaction that we had come safely through all nature's obstacles and also those of humans, particularly the dacoits. The locals in Mergui told us how a battalion of Burma Rifles was withdrawn by sea in the last week of December 1941, after the nearby tin and wolfram (tungsten) mines were put out of action by the Japanese. Even though many ragged Burmese soldiers were seen straggling in the streets, it appeared that the Burmese appointed by the Japanese army were running the government nominally. We also learned during our stay that there were some Australian prisoners of war working in camps at Ye and Tavoy.

To leave Mergui, one had to obtain a pass from the Burmese administration, which was possible only when someone could vouch for an applicant's credentials; but we did not know anybody in Mergui, who could do this for us. However, we managed to find a shopkeeper, named Prem Chand, who stood as a guarantor for us as men of good character. Since this gentleman had been so good to us we disclosed to him that we were going to India. He gave us letters to his relatives to be posted in India. Kaka, the Muslim servant of Khan Zaman, who had continued with us through our adventures, stayed behind in Mergui with people of his community from south India, who are called Kala (black) by the Burmese.

We left for Tavoy on 15 June 1942, once we had the permits to leave Mergui. The journey involved a bus and a boat. We were checked by the Japanese at many places and were asked the usual routine questions, such as our names, where we came from, where we were going, and were finally allowed to pass through. Incidentally, we had changed our vocations by this time and were now clerks of the Tabolick tin mines. We reached Tavoy in the evening of 16 June and stayed again in a Gurudwara. It was crowded with refugees who had lost their homes and property when the Japanese over-ran Burma. People talked about how the Japanese came and drove back the troops, even though there was no apparent damage to Tavoy. People from all walks of life were there and rumors of all sorts were common. Nobody questioned us about our identities or intentions. However, we were able to obtain a fair idea of the conditions in the area, which we would confront during the next stage of our trek. This helped us greatly in preparing our stories in case of an interrogation either by the Burmese police or the Japanese.

The next day, traveling by ferry and bus we reached Ye in the evening of 18 June. Once again we stayed in a Gurudwara. We next planned to go to Moulmein, but no transport was running in that direction as the bridge on the route had been destroyed. We therefore had to walk along the railway line. This was a very painful march as our shoes were completely worn out in the long 22-mile trek to Lamang, where we managed to board a train to Moulmein. Along the way we saw relics of vehicles abandoned by the retreating troops. As usual we stayed in a Gurudwara.

Pritam Singh and I were taken ill, but were fortunate to get treatment and medicines from a hospital run by missionaries. By the time we had recovered from our illness our money was almost spent. We approached Arjun Singh, a rich wood contractor and shop owner, and a known philanthropist who built the local Gurudwara. We revealed for the first time our adventures and identities, in the hope that he would give us a generous amount of money. To our great disappointment, he offered us only five Rupees, which we refused, greatly regretting the blunder we had made in revealing our identities.

There were four stragglers from the 8th Burma Rifles staying and working in the Gurudwara. We came to know that they wanted to go to India and told them that we would like to accompany them. We all left Moulmein on 30 June by ferry to Martaban. From there we went on foot along the railway tracks, then in country boats, and even in a cycle rickshaw, eventually reaching Pegu via Thaton village. The bridge over the Sitang River had been destroyed by our troops during the fierce fighting that had taken place. There were very few vehicles for hire and priority for seats was always given to the Burmese. We received many beatings for refusing to get out of buses, even though we had been given seats earlier than the Burmese who wanted them. Wishing to avoid any complications, we had to take these beatings without retaliating, and in most cases, without getting any seats. We stayed at Pegu for a day or two and then left for Rangoon.

On arrival at Rangoon on 4 July we all went to a Gurudwara. Here, the four men of the Burma Rifles decided not to go to India. This put us once again into financial difficulties. We stayed in the Gurudwara for about a week, but then realized that it would be risky to continue doing so as Rangoon was full of Japanese agents and there was a lot of activity. Besides, we met an Indian Sepoy driving a Japanese staff car, who asked us whether we had come from Singapore. These circumstances forced us to leave the Gurudwara. We went to Manigaon, near the Mingaladon airfield on the Prome road, about three miles outside of Rangoon.

We had been warned that we should keep away from wandering Burmese monks. These holy men wielded influence in Burma as they collaborated with the Japanese. Similarly, the extremist Thakin Party[29] was openly siding with the Japanese. Thus, it was difficult to know who was friendly with the Japanese and who was anti-Japanese. The uneducated masses appeared to be indifferent. The Karens[30] in the

[29] A Burmese nationalist group which was formed in the 1930s and comprised of young disgruntled intellectuals. Thakins were credited with the formation of the Burma National Army in 1942.

[30] An ethnic group who spoke a Sino-Tibetian language and lived primarily in the southern and southeastern part of Burma.

south and the hill people of the north seemed to be pro-British and did not readily act as agents or spies for the Japanese. However, they had not liked the scorched earth policy of the British when the latter withdrew from Burma. There were quite a large number of Indians at Manigaon, and we stayed in a deserted Gurudwara there. Since there was no *Granthi*[31] at the Gurudwara, Pritam Singh officiated as one on the occasion of the wedding of a Sikh couple. We enjoyed the wedding feast and had good food to eat after many days.

In Rangoon there was an office of the India Independence League. All the Indians in Rangoon were supposed to be members of the League. No passes or railway tickets could be obtained for leaving Rangoon unless one was a member. We therefore became members on the payment of one Rupee each.

From Rangoon, there were two possible routes leading to India: one via Prome and Sandoway in Arakan, and the other via Mandalay and Kalewa. The first route was shorter, but from Sandoway onward it was difficult to get drinking water; and we also heard that the Arakan coastal strip was carefully watched by the Japanese. Hence, we decided to go by the longer route, via Mandalay, Monywa and Kalewa. Our decision to take this route was also influenced by a chance conversation we had with a retired Sub-Inspector of Police, Pritam Singh from Monywa, who used to trade between Monywa and Rangoon. He gave us the details of the route to take.

While staying at Manigaon we tried to collect some money. Pritam Singh and Balbir Singh rendered assistance to a Sindhi merchant who was performing a religious ceremony, the Akhand Path.

---

[31] The person who reads the Guru Granth Sahib, the holy spiritual book of the Sikhs, in a Gurudwara.

In return they were given monetary reward. Also, we learned that Jemadar Ram Swarup, who used to be in my battalion's Intelligence, was with the small INA party posted there. We contacted him without knowing what his reaction would be, but he was very helpful and respectful. He gave us some money after we related our adventures to him. Eventually we collected about Rupees 200 and left by train for Mandalay on 9 August. On arriving in Mandalay we found that a large portion of the town had been destroyed. We stayed there for some days with a Sikh bullock cart owner.

We crossed the Irrawady River by boat and reached Monywa on 13 August. In Monywa we again met Pritam Singh, who was anxious to go to India but he had a Burmese wife who was not keen to leave Burma. A cousin of Pritam Singh, named Prem Singh was a very hospitable farmer; we took our baths at his house, even though we were staying in the Gurudwara. Prem Singh's younger brother appeared to have genuine interest in the people of India, and he gave us all the local information about the Japanese and the people living in the area. On a couple of occasions at Prem Singh's house, we met some South Indian people and refugee engineers who also were anxious to return to India, but their family obligations kept them in Monywa. We also heard that a number of Indians there from southern Burma tried to go to India, but many of them died of dysentery and other diseases en route. Those who survived their illnesses were looted and killed by Burmese dacoits. Clearly, Indians were not treated fairly by the Burmese.

In order to be able to trade in Burma, Indians were required to have business passes from Rangoon, upon the recommendation of the India Independence League. Further, they also had to obtain permission of the Japanese to cross the Chindwin River. We applied for a pass, stating that our parents had been stranded at Mawlaik and that we were going to fetch them back. However, the Japanese agreed to allow only two of us to go, while one would remain behind. We, therefore, gave up the idea of getting permits from them. In Monywa there were a number of Manipuris who had come from Mingan to get salt. We decided to join this party on their return journey early one morning.

At that time, a moderately built Sikh, Thakur Singh, had come to Monywa to open a branch of the India Independence League. He had Japanese newspapers published in English, which we borrowed; this association with him proved unfortunate for us. On 30 August, we left the Gurudwara early in the morning. We were sitting in a launch boat ready to cross the Chindwin River when Thakur Singh came to the riverfront with a Burmese policeman; they would not allow us to leave. He behaved in the most oppressive manner and used abusive language. He considered himself to be the most humble servant of Nippon. We begged him to leave us alone and asked him of his intentions for making such a scene at a public place. "Look brother, we are in a hell of a jam," said Pritam Singh, but Thakur Singh behaved in a disgusting manner. He became very excited and would not allow us to proceed. We had been terribly betrayed and we were deeply depressed. Every time we were in such situations, we consoled ourselves by saying, "while there is life there is a hope." Leaving the policeman to guard us, Thakur Singh went to report to a nearby Japanese officer.

Thakur Singh came back an hour later with a Japanese Intelligence officer. Unfortunately, this was the same officer who had earlier refused to allow the three of us to leave Monywa together. So naturally his suspicions were aroused. Our meager baggage was searched but nothing untoward was found. However, the fact that we had previously applied for passes convinced him that our credentials were not genuine. We were arrested and taken to the police station. In the meantime, the Burmese police had fetched the Japanese Military Police. The Japanese Intelligence Officer had decided that we must die. He drew his sword to kill us, when the Military Police Officer stopped him saying it was not the duty of the Intelligence Department, but that of the Military Police to deal with suspects. The Japanese Police wanted to extract information from us. This led to an argument between the Burmese Police and the Japanese, which saved us from immediate death.

During this interlude, I smoked as many Burmese cheroots as I could, thinking that they would not be needed any more; they were really soothing. I wanted to prepare myself for the terrible punishment of death. I requested the permission of the guard to allow me urgently to go to the latrine. There I chewed and swallowed some papers that could have been incriminating. During all interrogation we consistently maintained our story that we were from Pegu, that our parents had left for Mawlaik when the bombing occurred, and that they were now in great difficulty. The Military Police Officer appeared to be reasonable, but Thakur Singh wanted to know why we could not speak the Burmese language having lived in Pegu for so long. The Officer said that he would verify our story. We were then placed in separate confinement cells. While this was taking place, some members of the INA arrived in the town; then we were afraid that our identities might be disclosed. However, after about a fortnight, on 14 September, the Japanese Military Police Officer allowed us to leave the police station on the condition that we return to Pegu. He gave us our passes to return to Pegu.

When the news of our arrest had spread, a lot of Indians felt unhappy. Some even had heard that all three of us had been killed. We learned that the President of the local India Independence League had interceded on our behalf at his personal risk.

The moment we arrived at the Gurudwara, we were surrounded by our well-wishers. Our friends in the Gurudwara congratulated us on our luck and were wild with delight. We were very happy that we were free to leave Monywa. Of course, our intention was not to return to Pegu, but to try some other route to India before the Japanese changed their minds.

We decided to take the Myitkyina – Fort Hertz (Putao) route. It was a difficult, but not an impossible route. Pritam Singh did not agree with our plan as he thought that we were taking a lot of risk. He therefore decided to remain in a Sikh village named Chaungu, near Monywa. Later he came to India with Captain Mahabir Dhillon of the INA. We bade goodbye to Pritam, our companion during this long trek, who had accompanied us so courageously for more than four months. This struggle for our liberty had bound us together in close friendship. Pritam was a tall and well-built man, a tower of strength to us. I had found that men with the most impressive physique often were the first to crumble in the face of danger, whereas the least impressive ones often turned out to be stalwarts. However, Pritam was an exception to this, and he also had many other good qualities.

CHAPTER IX
LAST STRUGGLE TO FREEDOM

WE OBTAINED OUR PERMITS to leave Monywa through Mr. Pillai of the Public Works Department and took the train to Myitkyina, although we could only go as far as Yataung as the rail transport beyond was reserved solely for the use of Japanese troops. Fortunately, the Japanese Railway Station Master took pity on us and allowed us to travel by train to Myitkyina. The train carried Japanese troops in carriages, while equipment, supplies, and civilian passengers in open wagons. Leaving Yataung on 17 September 1942, we reached Myitkyina on 19 September.

To substantiate our story that we were businessmen, we purchased some small items, such as soap, in which we were supposed to be trading. Nothing unusual happened as far as Myitkyina, except normal checking by the Japanese and our suffering the usual harassment from Burmese civilians. At Myitkyina, we stayed with the relatives of a Sikh, who we had met in Monywa and who had directed us to stay with them. We met another Sikh, Bahadur Singh, who was the president of the newly formed India Independence League in that town. We took him into confidence, and on his advice, we approached the Japanese military authority at Myitkyina to get permits to proceed to Fort Hertz (Putao) under the pretext of meeting our parents and relatives stranded there. The Japanese gave us the permits. In Myitkyina we met some INA personnel, although we usually tried to avoid the members of the INA for fear of being recognized as escaped prisoners of war. At this meeting, one of the VCOs of the 4/19th

Hyderabad, Jemadar Uttam Singh, recognized me; however, he cordially, though secretly, gave us a warm welcome and much assistance with food.

Myitkyina is a rail head situated on the banks of the mighty Irrawady River. It had a good airfield, and the British hoped that it would provide a staging post between Assam State in India and China (Kunming). However, Myitkyina was occupied by the Japanese in May 1942, which posed great difficulties in ferrying supplies to China. All aircraft had to fly directly to Kunming at a distance of 500 miles over the mountains. This route later came to be known as the Hump. It passed over mountain peaks 15,000 feet high, and was considered to be the most difficult route in the world at that time. We saw these aircraft going over our heads.

We thought about going to Kunming along the Burma Road, via Bhamo – Namhkhan – Wanting on the border of China. We considered this possibility of going to China because we were told at Myitkyina that there was a dense jungle between India and Fort Hertz (Putao), which was impassable. We felt that it would be a thrilling experience to try to go to Kunming and then to India, but we were distrustful of the Chinese attitude. It was also difficult to distinguish the Chinese from the Japanese. After careful consideration, we decided to try our luck via Fort Hertz, as there would be better chances of making our escape good by remaining close to India. And so far, our trust in fate had not failed us.

We left for Fort Hertz on foot on 23 September and arrived at Kawapong that evening. On the way we met some Japanese troops and Burmese villagers walking along the trail. This trail was used previously by Chinese stragglers retreating from Burma. On the second night we stopped next to a Japanese camp occupied by an officer and some soldiers. We boldly approached them while they were having their meal. They hospitably offered us some boiled rice and grain of the type given in rations to our mules. Since we were very wet, the Japanese were kind enough to allow us to stay for the night in one of their shelters.

Prior to the war in Malaya, as stated earlier, there was a general belief that the Japanese were not good fighters. Besides, they had been fighting China since 1937, but had not been able to defeat the ill-equipped and poorly armed Chinese. This may have given rise to erroneous opinions of the capabilities of the Japanese; but we had learned quickly, at great cost, that the Japanese were among the best fighters in the world. They were extremely tough and stubborn fighters. Their loyalty to their emperor was intense. They were also frugal and good at improvisation, and could live on practically anything they found in the countryside. Normally, a Japanese soldier was issued with rice and salted fish that could last for a week. Similarly, an adequate supply of small arms ammunition and hand grenades was supplied to them. All this was either put in a pack or tied in a waterproof bundle, which the Japanese soldier carried on his back. While operating in a jungle or wet country, he wore a loincloth. Japanese were not very particular about wearing uniforms and were often in civilian clothes. Whenever the Japanese soldier found time, he boiled rice in his ration tin, together with some tender leaves or shoots found in the jungles. These practices improved their mobility, individual initiative, and the ability to overcome difficulties quickly. The Japanese also took great delight in fishing and photography.

The Japanese soldiers were remarkable people. They accepted

punishment without any grumbling. Curiously enough, beating and slapping were the usual forms of punishment. Normally, the Japanese were found to be temperamental and short tempered, yet they never protested against living conditions or non-existence of welfare arrangements. In peacetime they were seen to be extremely polite; they paid respect by bowing to their friends and elders. But, they were most barbarous and cruel in war. They showed great pleasure in torturing innocent prisoners of war or suspect Chinese. Usually, they tied their prisoners' hands and bayoneted them to death.

Continuing our journey the next day, we spent the third night (after leaving Myitkyina by foot) in a deserted hut near a deserted village. We were told that the villagers had fled at the time of the Chinese retreat along this route. Although we passed several Japanese posts on the fourth day, nothing of interest took place.

On the fifth day, we thought that we would see no more Japanese posts; but towards the evening, we suddenly came across a Japanese detachment of about 40 strong, billeted in a *dak* bungalow[32]. They were commanded by an officer, and the party also had a doctor. They would not allow us to proceed, and sent a wireless message to Myitkyina asking for instructions. The reply came through saying that we should be brought back to Myitkyina. The Japanese officer told us that we will be taken back to Myitkyina the next day when they would be withdrawing. They allowed us to remain in a small part of the building they had occupied. The news that we would have to return to Myitkyina upset us very much, as it would involve further enquiries into our movements, and also would reveal our

[32] A house built by British government for travelers to stay. Also used as vacation home by British government officials.

unsuccessful bid to cross the Chindwin River. We could not discuss our plans at any length as such discussions would have been overheard and given cause for more suspicion. We finally decided that under no circumstances would we return with the Japanese, but would try somehow to give them the slip.

Early next morning, before dawn, the Japanese moved off in two parties. We were left with the second party commanded by an NCO; the doctor was with this party. While walking along, aided by the darkness of the early morning, we managed to give our Japanese companions the slip and went into the jungle. Believing that we were not likely to meet any more Japanese posts, we were moving as fast as we could, urged on by the fear of recapture and the resultant punishment that would be nothing less than death. I was in the lead and suddenly came across a solitary Japanese sentry warming himself near a fire. There was no time to lose; prompt action was necessary. I signaled to Balbir Singh to halt. I greeted the sentry in his own language. He however took little, if any, notice of me. We managed to slip past him without arousing his suspicions. Once we had passed this sentry, we increased our pace to almost running.

At about mid-day, we were suddenly stopped by some troops on patrol dressed in unidentifiable uniform, but armed with our service rifles. Their leader took us to his commander who fortunately spoke Hindustani. After a while, we recognized each other as we had attended a training course together at Belgaum, India; at that time he was with the Burma Rifles. From him we learned that the troops belonged to the Kachin Levies[33]. We told this officer our story and requested him to take us to his headquarters at Sumprabum. We gave him as much information as we could about the Japanese posts.

The Kachin Levies was a force, organized from the hill people along the eastern frontier, to undertake guerilla operations against the Japanese lines of communications, should they pass through that area. This force later came to be known as the "Y" Force, and its original role was gradually changed to that of obtaining information about the Japanese Army, which had not followed up on its success in Burma. In addition, the Force provided guides and porters, and became a link between the British Army and the local inhabitants, who could not understand how the Japanese, half-naked and half starved, drove away the "invincible white man!"

The leader of the Kachin Levies sent us to a village with two men of his party. We had to climb a very steep hill to reach this village. In spite of our fatigue we managed it. That night we had good food with the Kachin villagers. In our honor a chicken was cooked in spices. We ate the chicken despite the fact that pounded cockroaches were used for its seasoning. These people were extremely poor. They had Mongolian features with slit eyes, and lived simply and naturally. Their health seemed poor, but they were proud people. They were unable to read or write, but were well aware of what was happening in the outside world.

To travel to Sumprabum we did not follow the track that would

---

[33] A special force created by the British during World War II in Burma. The Levies were made up of members of the Kachin peoples under the command of British army officers. They fought the Japanese in the jungles of Northern Burma. Major Edmund Leech set up the Levies at Fort Hertz in Burma and Colonel Gamble was the commandant of the Levies.

have been a much shorter route, but had to go from village to village. We had many hills to climb and many creeks and very swift streams to cross. The Kachin villages are normally located on the top of the hills and the houses are made of bamboos. While crossing a stream, Balbir Singh slipped, fell, and lost the bundle he was carrying. We were worried lest he was swept away by the swift current. Fortunately, he managed to grasp a hanging creeper and save himself; but he lost his clothes and our cooking pot, which we wanted to keep as a souvenir.

Incidentally, thousands of refugees from northern Burma, especially the Myitkyina area, made their way on foot via this route, the Hukawng Valley, and from Fort Hertz over the Chaukan Pass to Ledo. Many refugees who attempted this longer and more difficult route suffered a great deal and died on the way.

The remnants of the Chinese V Army also made their way along this track. They had behaved like Chengiz Khan's hoards. They looted and robbed the locals of their food and fowls. The local tribes managed to kill some of them in retribution for their acts of violence.

When we arrived at Sumprabum, we met Commander Major Leech, who received us in the friendliest manner, in spite of our appearance that was anything but officer-like. He accepted our story without any reservation. Our arrival coincided with a supply by airdrop to the headquarters; and as a result, we wined and dined most sumptuously that night. Major Leech passed on the information of our arrival to Lieutenant Colonel Gamble, who was coming from Fort Hertz to Sumprabum, and who conveyed this information to the headquarters of the IV Corps. After being well fed and rested for a few days to allow our depleted energy level to recover, we were transported on elephant to Fort Hertz. The most popular currency in Sumprabum was silver coins, and Major Leech gave us a couple of handfuls of Rupee coins. Nobody could have been kinder and more hospitable than Major Leech. The coolies and mahouts employed by the Kachin Levies were usually paid in opium or salt. These addicts were given a daily quota of opium that was dropped by air.

We reached Fort Hertz after three days and met Colonel Gamble. There was a landing strip there, and shortly after our arrival, we saw a Dakota aircraft landing. There was no road communication between Fort Hertz and India. A company of a Jat battalion had been flown in the first week of September to Fort Hertz to protect the landing ground. This was done to raise and support the Kachin Levies operating against the Japanese. We were fortunate as we were given a lift in an aircraft and taken to Tinsukia (Assam, India) on 6 October.

We were thrilled to be on Indian soil again after trekking through Malaya, Thailand and Burma over a period of five months and two days. We had covered a distance of at least 3000 miles, on foot, by train, in boat, in bullock cart, and so on. Thus ended the hazardous and intense physical and mental trials. From Tinsukia we were taken to Dibrugarh in a truck driven by an African American. He was a good driver, but we were flung about in the body of the bouncing truck. We spent the night in Dibrugarh and went to Jorhat, the headquarters of the IV Corps, the following day. We were interrogated at the Corps headquarters by General Wavell, Commander-in-Chief India, who happened to be on tour. He listened to our narration carefully without revealing his opinions. We thought, he would say that we ran faster than others, but were proven wrong! He congratulated us on our stout efforts. We were told that he rarely congratulated anyone.

We were given uniforms and field checkbooks. At that time a number of Japanese agents were arriving in India; we therefore aroused strong suspicions. At Jorhat we were placed under a guard of the Marathas. Even though it was not mentioned to us, the Maratha battalion had orders to watch over us. This dampened our spirits and we protested strongly, but we did not know what effect that had. A few days later we were sent to Calcutta, to the headquarters of the Eastern Army at Barrackpore, with a Lieutenant Colonel of the Gurkha Rifles as an escort, which again was not made obvious. The Army Commander was Lieutenant General Irwin, who interviewed us. At Calcutta, I was admitted to the Military Hospital at Barrackpore for malaria treatment, and Captain Balbir Singh was sent to Delhi, where I joined him after about a fortnight. By this time, Captain Pritam Singh had also arrived; and a complete interrogation of the three of us was carried out at the Red Fort in Delhi. We were then sent to our Training Center at Agra in November 1942. A few days later I went on leave.

The first telegram I sent home informing my family of my safe return was from Dimapur (Assam), the place of a large transit camp. My relatives did not believe that the telegram was a genuine one and were convinced only when they received a letter from me, which I had sent from the Military Hospital in Calcutta. Fifteen years later, when I visited the Dimapur post office, it was in the same condition as when I first saw it at the time of sending the telegram home.

It is the duty of every prisoner of war to try to escape, even though this cannot be achieved without taking some risks. In our own escape efforts we had often differed in our plans, and it was mighty difficult for all three of us to come to a consensus. It was always a compromise. In difficult circumstances, when tempers were strained and nerves were on an edge, it was only too easy to quarrel with each other. In recklessness we may not have adopted an optimal plan; but having agreed to one, we always carried it out with determination. With patience and tolerance we emerged successful and in high spirits. Greater than all these qualities in the circumstances was possession of guts and faith; faith in the ultimate success.

Let me pay tribute to my companions, to our colleagues who were left in the prisoner-of-war camp, and to others who helped us at the peril of their lives by giving money, shelter and advice. Balbir Singh was a wonderful person and an excellent companion. He was wiry and tough, with physical and moral courage of the highest order. He stood to the cause and by his friends under all hardships. He was a gallant soldier and a thorough gentleman.

On our return from leave, the three of us were showered with considerable praise and attention, and made to feel much greater than we knew ourselves to be. The crowning event took place in February 1943, when we were awarded the Military Cross, the prestigious award for gallantry, by the British Viceroy in India during a grand ceremonial parade at the large square on Rajpath in New Delhi.

TIMELINE OF EVENTS AND ESCAPE MILESTONES

April 1940	Second Lieutenant Gangaram Parab join 4th Battalion of the 19th Hyderabad Regiment (4/19th Hyderabad), and are shipped out to Singapore.
December 8, 1941	Hostilities (code named "Gloves Off") between the Japanese and the Allies commence. Singapore and Kota Bharu, Malaya are bombed by the Japanese. Japanese land on Kota Bharu beaches.
9 December 1941	4/19th Hyderabad reaches Kuala Krai, Malaya.
10 December 1941	Japanese airplanes attack 4/19th Hyderabad.
11 December 1941	8 Brigade and 4/19th Hyderabad are given orders to withdraw.
13–31 December 1941	British troops withdraw to Gopeng, Bidor and Slim River area (Malaya).
1 January 1942	Seven Japanese steamships and barges land at the mouth of the Bernam River, Malaya.
6–7 January 1942	Battle of Slim River takes place.
30–31 January 1942	British troops finally withdraw from

	Malaya peninsula.
5 February 1942	Japanese bomb Singapore Island. The ship "Empress of India", a troop transport vessel, is sunk.
8 February 1942	Japanese begin shelling Singapore Island.
15 February 1942	Singapore surrenders to the Japanese troops.
4 May 1942	Gangaram Parab, Balbir Singh, and Pritam Singh escape from the Japanese prisoner-of-war camp in Singapore. They begin journey to India.
6 May 1942	Escapees reach Prai and Alor Star in Malaya.
22 May 1942	Escapees leave for Padang Besar (near the Malayan border) and the village of Haadyai, Thailand.
25 May 1942	Escapees reach Bandon, Thailand.
26 May 1942	Escapees arrive at Chumphon, Thailand.
27 May 1942	Escapees arrive at Prachuap Khiri Khan, Thailand.
1 June 1942	Escapees leave Prachuap Khiri Khan, Thailand, and they travel through the jungles of the Tenasserim region in Thailand and Burma.
5 June 1942	Escapees reach Tabolik, Burma.
10 June 1942	Escapees reach Mergui, Burma.

15 June 1942	Escapees leave for Tavoy, Burma.
16 June 1942	Escapees reach Tavoy, Burma.
18 June 1942	Escapees arrive in Ye, Burma, by ferry and bus.
19 June 1942	Escapees leave Ye, and walk 22 miles along railway tracks to Lamang, Burma.
24 June 1942	Escapees reach Moulmein, Burma, by train.
30 June 1942	Escapees leave Moulmein by ferry to Martaban; then travel by foot along railway tracks, then in country boats, towards Pegu via Thaton.
2 July 1942	Escapees arrive in Pegu, Burma.
4 July 1942	Escapees arrive in Rangoon, Burma.
9 August 1942	Escapees leave Rangoon area for Mandalay, Burma.
13 August 1942	Escapees arrive in Monywa, Burma.
30 August 1942	Escapees are arrested by the Japanese Military police and put in jail.
14 September 1942	Escapees are released from jail and are put on a train back to Pegu, Burma.
15 September 1942	Escapees decide to split up. Gangaram Parab and Balbir Singh proceed ahead to India, while Pritam Singh stays in Monywa to return separately.
17 September 1942	Gangaram Parab and Balbir Singh

	travel to Yataung, Burma.
19 September 1942	Gangaram Parab and Balbir Singh reach Myitkyina, Burma.
23 September 1942	Gangaram Parab and Balbir Singh walk to Kawapong on their way to Fort Hertz, Burma.
30 September 1942	Gangaram Parab and Balbir Singh are assisted by the Kachin Levies Scouts and brought to Sumprabum, Burma.
3 October 1942	Gangaram Parab and Balbir Singh are transported on elephant to Fort Hertz.
6 October 1942	Gangaram Parab and Balbir Singh arrive at Fort Hertz, and are flown to Tinsukia, India. This ends their escape from the Japanese prisoner-of-war camp Singapore after trekking through Malaya, Thailand and Burma for a period of five months and two days.
February 1943	Gangaram Parab, Balbir Singh, and Pritam Singh are awarded the Military Cross for gallantry and distinguished service in the field.

A GALLANT SOLDIER PASSES AWAY

MANY BRAVE AND HEROIC MEN AND WOMEN have made the prime sacrifice of their own lives while serving the ideals of their motherland. On 21 January 1973, yet another of these stars, bright and even young, was suddenly eclipsed for all time to come.

Major Anil G. Parab of the renowned 4th Battalion of the Kumaon Regiment was in charge of a battalion field firing conducted for the purpose of testing weapons and preparing the unit for further operations. After firing all other weapons it was time to fire the 3.5 inch rocket launchers. Major Parab himself first fired the rocket launcher to prove the serviceability of the weapon. He then ordered the detachment commanders to continue the firing. The third shell fired fell short and Major Parab, who was watching the firing from a trench, was hit in the chest by a small splinter that killed him instantaneously. There was no chance to give him any medical aid.

Twenty-six year old Major Parab was the only son of Colonel Gangaram S. Parab, MC and Sulabha Parab. He came from a family with high military traditions. From his very childhood, Anil wanted to follow in the footsteps of his illustrious fore-fathers. At the age of ten, he stood first in the competitive examination for the Prince of Wales Royal Military College, Dehra Dun, and was offered a scholarship for the complete duration of this training by the State of Maharashtra. It was very difficult to dissuade the boy from going away to Dehra Dun at such a tender age; however, on the advice of the Principal of The Bishop School, Poona, Anil agreed to defer his decision to pursue military training until after completing High School and the Senior Cambridge Examination.

While at The Bishop School, Anil persevered with great zeal and excelled not only in the class room but also in sports and other extra-curricular activities. He captained the school cricket, football, hockey and swimming teams, and took great interest in scouting. Very fittingly, he was selected as the Head-Boy of the school and had the honor of winning the coveted Governor's Cup for the Best All-Round Student, and the "Rex Ludorum" award.

Anil was among the top candidates in the 1963 National Defence Academy (NDA) entrance examination and did exceedingly well at the NDA. He won several trophies and held high leadership appointments. After successfully completing the three-year training there, he entered the Indian Military Academy, Dehra Dun. There

Anil attained the position of Battalion Under Officer. At the end of the training in 1967, he placed fifth in the order of merit among 350 cadets, and was wooed by all the units to join their regiments. Anil opted to join the famous 4th Battalion of the Kumaon Regiment, the one in which his father also fought and was decorated for gallantry. This Regiment has produced several Generals and two Chiefs of Army Staff. Inspired by the heroic deeds of the Battalion, the young officer did his best to uphold the good name and the tradition of the 4th Kumaon. On every Army course he obtained only the top-most results. Similarly, he showed his prowess in other fields. His high sense of duty and team-spirit earned him a good name and popularity with his "paltan". His sense of discipline was of the highest order.

In 1971, Captain Parab was an instructor at the Indian Army Counter Insurgency and Jungle Warfare School in Vairengte, Mizoram. When call of the Nation came for action in Bangla Desh, he was seriously ill and being treated in the hospital for a liver infection arising from difficult living conditions in the jungles. The doctors would not allow him to rejoin the Unit. However, his restless mind could not keep silent and he successfully persuaded the medical specialist to permit him to participate in the war. There he went out leading his band of grand men with confidence and courage to breach the defences of the enemy. His daring action, which was many a time at the peril of his life, contributed significantly towards liberating Bangla Desh. Indeed, he was a modern-day Abhimanyu!

On 21 January 1973, this shining star was snuffed forever. Anil Parab's near and dear ones were left to silently bear with as much courage as sorrow this grave and irreparable loss. Others have been left with a shining specimen of a young and promising man who was dedicated to the cause of the Country. His loss would not go in vain if the example set by him is emulated by others. In August 1973, Major Anil Parab was posthumously awarded the "Naga Hills" Medal for gallantry.

A GLOSSARY OF SELECTED MILITARY TERMS

Battalion: A military unit containing 300–1300 soldiers, which is led by a Lieutenant Colonel. A battalion consists of two to seven companies.

Brigade: A major tactical military formation usually composed of three to six battalions, which is commanded by a Brigadier, Brigadier General, or a Colonel. A brigade may contain 3000–5000 soldiers.

Brigade Major: The Chief of Staff of a brigade, whose role was to expand, detail, and execute the orders of the Commanding Brigadier.

Company: A military unit composed of 80–225 soldiers, which is led by a Captain or Major. A company is composed of three to six platoons.

Division: A large military unit usually comprising between 10,000 and 30,000 soldiers. A division contains four brigades and is commanded by a Major General.

DSO: Distinguished Service Order, military award of the British Crown for distinguished service by officers of the armed forces during wartime, typically in actual combat.

Havaldar:	The rank of a Viceroy Commissioned Officer (VCO equivalent to a sargent).
Infantry:	The branch of the army, which fights on foot. It is the back bone of a modern army.
Jemadar:	The rank used in the British Indian Army for a soldier promoted from the ranks, usually after at least 10 years of service. This was the lowest rank for a Viceroy Commissioned Officer (VCO).
MC:	Military Cross, a prestigious medal awarded for acts of exemplary gallantry during operations against the enemy.
NCO:	Non-commissioned officer, a rank not commissioned in the Army, but which formed the backbone of the army. Senior NCOs were considered the primary link between enlisted personnel and the commissioned officers in a military organization. Their advice and guidance was particularly important for junior officers, who began their careers in a position of authority but generally lacked practical experience.
Platoon:	A military unit consisting of two to four sections or squadrons of about 26 to 64 soldiers. This is the smallest unit to be led by a commissioned officer called a Platoon Leader.

Regiment:	A military unit consisting of at least two battalions, usually commanded by a Colonel.
Sepoy:	A soldier.
Subedar:	The rank used in the British Indian Army for a senior Viceroy Commissioned Officer (VCO).
VCO:	Viceroy Commissioned Officer, an Indian soldier promoted from the ranks, usually after at least 10 years of service. VCOs were the principal link between the army's mostly British officers and the sepoys.

PHOTOGRAPHS

Presentation of Military Cross
at Ceremonial Parade in Delhi,
February 1943.

Receiving the Military Cross,
February 1943.

Major Rashid and Captain Parab
congratulating each other after
the Military Cross presentation ceremony, February 1943.

Col. Gangaram S. Parab, MC
in full military honor medals dress.

Medals, listing from left to right:
» Indian Independance 1947 » Military Cross 1943
» GRJ VI 1939–1945 Star » GRJ VI The Pacific Star
» GRJ VI The Burma Star » King George Defence Medal 1939–1945
» George VI 1939–1945

Numb. 35957

SUPPLEMENT
TO
The London Gazette
Of FRIDAY, the 26th of MARCH, 1943
Published by Authority

Registered as a newspaper

1459

TUESDAY, 30 MARCH, 1943

CENTRAL CHANCERY OF THE ORDERS
OF KNIGHTHOOD.

St. James's Palace, S.W.1, 30th March, 1943.

The KING has been graciously pleased to give orders for the following appointments to the Most Excellent Order of the British Empire, in recognition of gallant and distinguished services in the field:—

To be Additional Members of the Military Division of the said Most Excellent Order:—

Captain (temporary Major) Mahabir Singh Dhillon, Royal Indian Army Service Corps.
Second-Lieutenant Bakhtawar Singh, Corps of Indian Engineers (attached King George V's Own Bengal Sappers and Miners).

CENTRAL CHANCERY OF THE ORDERS
OF KNIGHTHOOD.

St. James's Palace, S.W.1, 30th March, 1943.

The KING has been graciously pleased, on the advice of Canadian Ministers, to approve the award of the George Medal, in recognition of conspicuous gallantry in carrying out hazardous work in a very brave manner, to:—

Lieutenant Edward Thomas Galway, The Corps of Royal Canadian Engineers.

CENTRAL CHANCERY OF THE ORDERS
OF KNIGHTHOOD.

St. James's Palace, S.W.1, 30th March, 1943.

The KING has been graciously pleased, on the advice of Canadian Ministers, to approve the award of the British Empire Medal (Military Division), in recognition of gallant conduct in carrying out hazardous work in a very brave manner, to:—

C.2358 Sapper John Lorraine, The Corps of Royal Canadian Engineers.

War Office, 30th March, 1943.

The KING has been graciously pleased to approve the following awards in recognition of gallant and distinguished services in the field:—

The Military Cross.

Lieutenant (temporary Captain) Pritam Singh, 16th Punjab Regiment, Indian Army.
Lieutenant (temporary Captain) Balbir Singh, 19th Hyderabad Regiment, Indian Army.
Lieutenant (temporary Captain) Gangaram Parab, 19th Hyderabad Regiment, Indian Army.

War Office, 30th March, 1943.

The KING has been graciously pleased to approve the following awards in recognition of gallant and distinguished services in the South West Pacific:—

The Military Cross.

Captain Basil Wilfrid Thomas Catterns (NX 342), Australian Military Forces.
Captain John Fletcher Connell (VX 13901), Australian Military Forces.
Lieutenant (temporary Captain) Russell Wilkinson Forster (QX 1253), Australian Military Forces.
Lieutenant Gordon Leslie Leaney (NX 34302), Australian Military Forces. (Since killed in action.)
Lieutenant Maurice George O'Donnell (WX 2406), Australian Military Forces.

The Distinguished Conduct Medal.

No. NX 4546 Sergeant Keith Carey, Australian Military Forces.
No. WX13036 Sergeant William O'Neill, Australian Military Forces.
No. QX38364 Corporal Clive Blair, Australian Military Forces.
No. NX 68711 Corporal Robert Ray Stoddart, Australian Military Forces.
No. VX 20960 Private Roy Hammond Marriott, Australian Military Forces.

The Military Medal.

No. QX 21559 Sergeant Malcolm Alexander Bishop, Australian Military Forces.
No. VX 31608 Sergeant Kenneth Harry Davy, Australian Military Forces.
No. QX 39623 Lance-Sergeant Colin Andrews, Australian Military Forces.
No. NX 9045 Lance-Sergeant John Doran, Australian Military Forces.
No. NX 28926 Corporal William Henry James Devine, Australian Military Forces.
No. VX 12331 Corporal Roland Brown Duncan, Australian Military Forces.
No. NX 42526 Corporal Herbert John Shearwin, Australian Military Forces.
No. V 230062 Lance-Corporal Edward Norman Butler, Australian Military Forces.
No. NX 1831 Lance-Corporal Joseph Christopher Mitchell, Australian Military Forces.
No. NX 72951 Lance-Corporal Christopher William Ward, Australian Military Forces.
No. QX 20028 Private Alfred Anderson, Australian Military Forces.
No. QX 12496 Private Hugh Charles Campbell, Australian Military Forces.
No. NX 41133 Private Norman Capel, Australian Military Forces. (Since deceased.)
No. NX 6271 Gunner Allan Gillies King, Australian Military Forces.

Excerpt from Supplement to The London Gazette
of Friday, the 26th of March 1943.

Painting of Regiment founder, Sir Henry Russell.
Kumaon Regimental Center Officers' Mess, Ranikhet.

Kumaon Regimental War Memorial, Ranikhet.

Wall with inscription at
the Kumaon Regimental War Memorial, Ranikhet.

"When you go home, tell them of us and say:
For your tomorrow, we gave our today."

Battle Honors Wall for various wars
fought by the Kumaon Battalions.
Kumaon Regimental War Memorial, Ranikhet,
October, 2010.

Memorial Wall with names of fallen heros.
Kumaon Regimental War Memorial, Ranikhet.

Aruna Seth with Brigadier Jasbir Singh, Commandant,
Kumaon Regimental Center, Ranikhet,
October 2010.

ACKNOWLEDGMENTS

We wish to express our deep gratitude to our niece, Mrs. Shilpa Desai, for designing this book and her valuable insights and assistance in publishing it.

We would also like to extend our thanks to Ms. Heather Reitze for her assistance in editing the manuscript.

7009849R00075

Printed in Great Britain
by Amazon.co.uk, Ltd.,
Marston Gate.